CHAPTER 25 Adding 3-Digit Numbers

Write as many addition problems as you can, using the numbers in the picture.

SCHOOL HOME CONNECTION

Dear Family,

Today we started Chapter 25. We will look at ways to add 3-digit numbers. Here is the math vocabulary and an activity for us to do together at home.

Love,

____

My Math Words

decimal point
dollar sign

Vocabulary

decimal point The dot in a money amount that separates dollars from cents.

dollar sign The symbol at the beginning of a money amount that shows dollars.

decimal point ↓

dollar sign → **$ 4.80**

Activity

With your child, look through newspaper ads to find two items priced between $1.00 and $4.99. Have your child use real money, if possible, to find the cost of buying both items. Repeat with other prices.

Books to Share

To read about adding 3-digit numbers with your child, look for these books in your local library.

The 329th Friend,
by Marjorie Weinman Sharmat,
Simon & Schuster, 1992.

The Purse,
by Kathy Caple,
Houghton Mifflin, 1992.

Visit *The Learning Site* for additional ideas and activities. www.harcourtschool.com

Name ______________________________

Add Hundreds

What is 300 + 100?

3 + 1 = 4

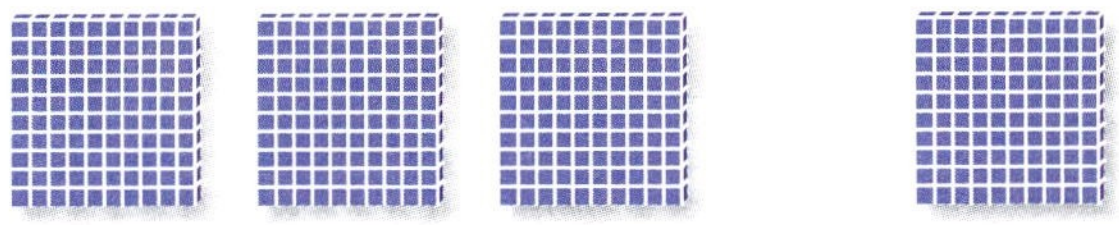

3 hundreds + 1 hundred = 4 hundreds 300 + 100 = 400

Add.

1. 5 + 4 = ______

   5 hundreds + 4 hundreds = ______ hundreds

   500 + 400 = ______

2. 3 + 5 = ______

   3 hundreds + 5 hundreds = ______ hundreds

   300 + 500 = ______

3. 6 + 0 = ______

   6 hundreds + 0 hundreds = ______ hundreds

   600 + 0 = ______

4. 5 + 2 = ______

   5 hundreds + 2 hundreds = ______ hundreds

   500 + 200 = ______

Talk About It ■ **Reasoning**

How does knowing the sum of 4 + 3 help you add 400 + 300?

Add.

1

2	2 hundreds	200
+ 4	+ 4 hundreds	+ 400
6	6 hundreds	600

2

4	4 hundreds	400
+ 5	+ 5 hundreds	+ 500
	hundreds	

3

1	1 hundred	100
+ 7	+ 7 hundreds	+ 700
	hundreds	

4

2	2 hundreds	200
+ 2	+ 2 hundreds	+ 200
	hundreds	

5

3	3 hundreds	300
+ 4	+ 4 hundreds	+ 400
	hundreds	

6

5	5 hundreds	500
+ 0	+ 0 hundreds	+ 0
	hundreds	

7

6	6 hundreds	600
+ 3	+ 3 hundreds	+ 300
	hundreds	

8

3	3 hundreds	300
+ 2	+ 2 hundreds	+ 200
	hundreds	

Algebra

Use the pattern to help you add.

9

4	40	400
+ 3	+ 30	+ 300

10

8	80	800
+ 1	+ 10	+ 100

HOME ACTIVITY • Put out 4 dollars and 5 dollars. Remind your child that each dollar is worth 100 cents. Ask your child to find 4¢ + 5¢ (9¢), then 400¢ + 500¢ (900¢). Repeat with other groups of dollars.

Name ______________________________

Model 3-Digit Addition

135 + 147 = ______

Step 1

Add the ones.
Regroup 12 ones to make 1 ten and 2 ones.
Write 1 in the tens column.

hundreds	tens	ones
	1	
1	3	5
+ 1	4	7
		2

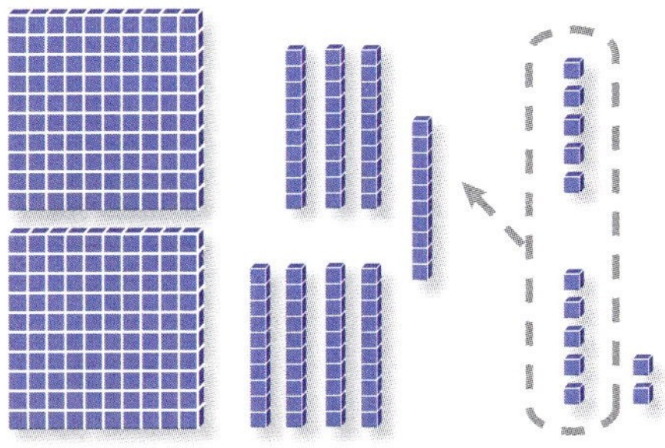

Step 2

Add the tens.
Write the number of tens.

hundreds	tens	ones
	1	
1	3	5
+ 1	4	7
	8	2

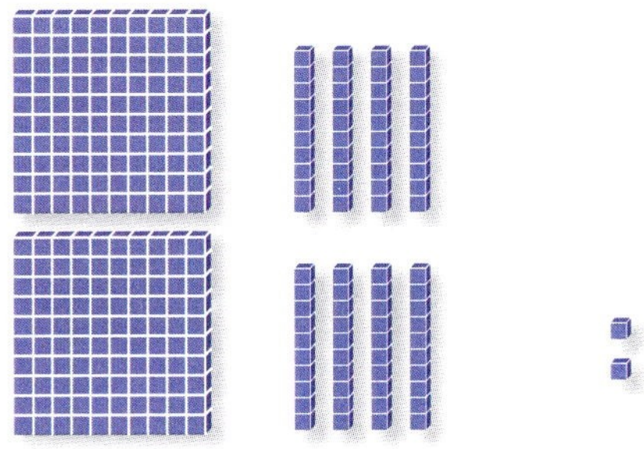

Step 3

Add the hundreds.
Write the number of hundreds.

hundreds	tens	ones
	1	
1	3	5
+ 1	4	7
2	8	2

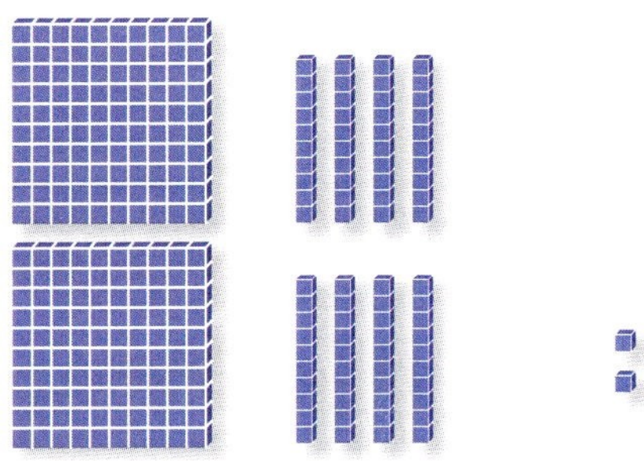

Use hundreds, tens, ones blocks. Add. Regroup if you need to.

1

hundreds	tens	ones
	☐	
6	4	5
+ 1	3	5

2

hundreds	tens	ones
	☐	
3	3	6
+ 2	2	7

3

hundreds	tens	ones
	☐	
4	6	1
+ 5	1	8

Talk About It ■ **Reasoning**

What would happen if you added the hundreds place first, the tens place second, and the ones place last?

Use hundreds, tens, ones blocks. Add. Regroup if you need to.

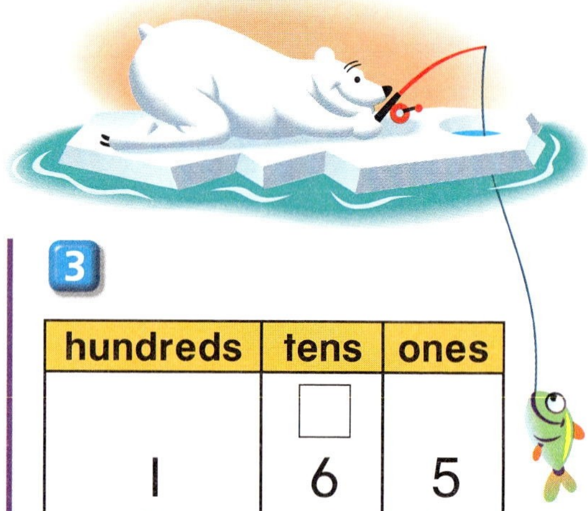

1

	hundreds	tens	ones
		1	
	2	1	9
+	2	5	4
	4	7	3

2

	hundreds	tens	ones
		☐	
	3	5	8
+	1	1	2

3

	hundreds	tens	ones
		☐	
	1	6	5
+	4	2	9

4

	hundreds	tens	ones
		☐	
	2	8	4
+	5	0	7

5

	hundreds	tens	ones
		☐	
	7	0	5
+	1	3	4

6

	hundreds	tens	ones
		☐	
	3	6	8
+		1	6

7

	hundreds	tens	ones
		☐	
	2	4	9
+	1	2	3

8

	hundreds	tens	ones
		☐	
	6	3	9
+	1	5	6

9

	hundreds	tens	ones
		☐	
	4	4	7
+	3	4	3

Problem Solving • Estimation

Estimate. Circle **greater than 500** or **less than 500**.

10 309 + 43

greater than 500
less than 500

11 232 + 693

greater than 500
less than 500

HOME ACTIVITY • Ask your child to tell you how he or she knows when to regroup. Use one of the problems on this page.

Name ______________________________

Add 3-Digit Numbers

142 + 185 = ______

Step 1

Add the ones.
Write the number of ones.

hundreds	tens	ones
☐	☐	
1	4	2
+ 1	8	5
		7

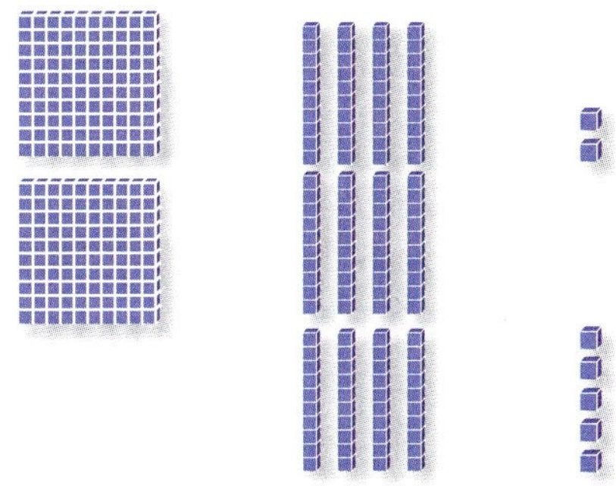

Step 2

Add the tens.
Regroup 12 tens as 1 hundred and 2 tens.
Write the number of tens.

hundreds	tens	ones
1	☐	
1	4	2
+ 1	8	5
	2	7

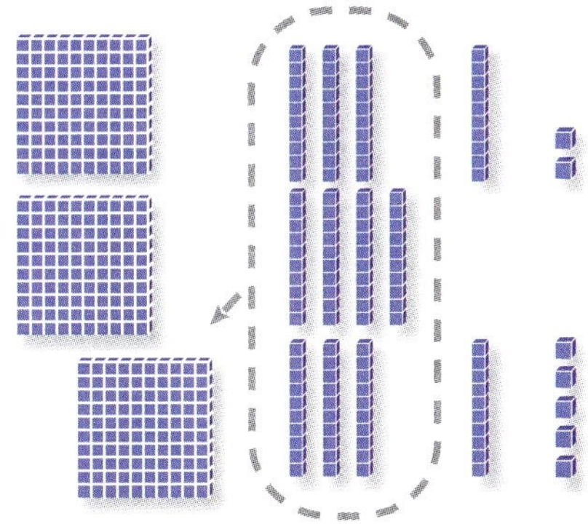

Step 3

Add the hundreds.
Write the number of hundreds.

hundreds	tens	ones
1	☐	
1	4	2
+ 1	8	5
3	2	7

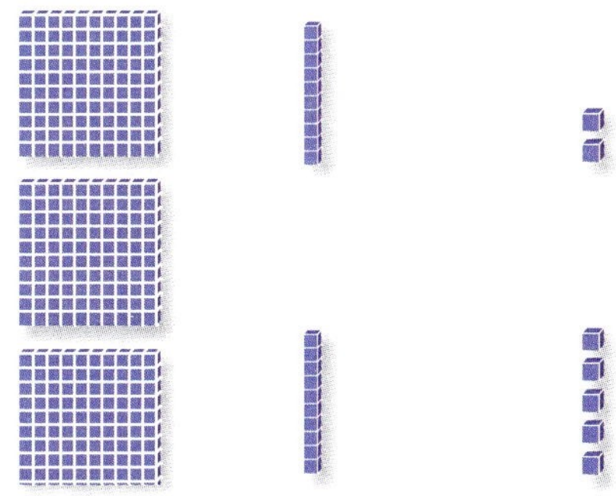

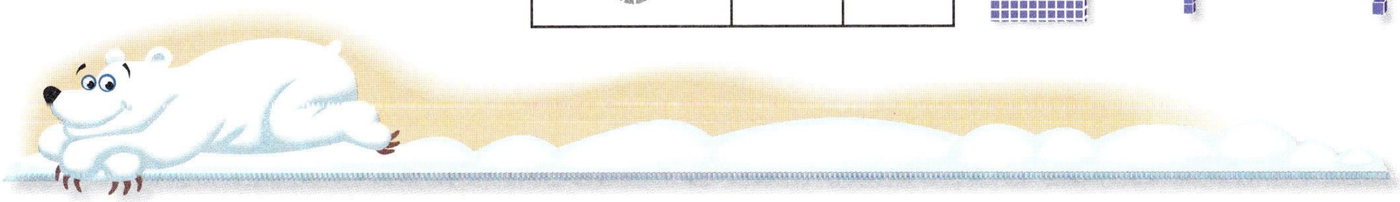

Add.

1

hundreds	tens	ones
☐	☐	
5	6	8
+ 2	5	0

2

hundreds	tens	ones
☐	☐	
6	7	7
+ 2	0	3

3

hundreds	tens	ones
☐	☐	
4	7	7
+ 1	4	2

Talk About It ■ Reasoning

Ann got 7118 as an answer for problem 1. What did she do wrong?

Add.

1

hundreds	tens	ones
□	□	
5	9	3
+ 2	8	6
8	7	9

2

hundreds	tens	ones
□	□	
3	2	9
+ 3	4	2

3

hundreds	tens	ones
□	□	
6	7	3
+ 2	3	4

4 $\begin{array}{r} 153 \\ +354 \\ \hline 507 \end{array}$

5 $\begin{array}{r} 132 \\ +622 \\ \hline \end{array}$

6 $\begin{array}{r} 408 \\ +356 \\ \hline \end{array}$

7 $\begin{array}{r} 710 \\ +197 \\ \hline \end{array}$

8 $\begin{array}{r} 238 \\ +559 \\ \hline \end{array}$

9 $\begin{array}{r} 463 \\ +374 \\ \hline \end{array}$

10 $\begin{array}{r} 953 \\ +\ \ 27 \\ \hline \end{array}$

11 $\begin{array}{r} 690 \\ +309 \\ \hline \end{array}$

12 $\begin{array}{r} 418 \\ +479 \\ \hline \end{array}$

13 $\begin{array}{r} 184 \\ +713 \\ \hline \end{array}$

14 $\begin{array}{r} 537 \\ +248 \\ \hline \end{array}$

15 $\begin{array}{r} 835 \\ +\ \ 94 \\ \hline \end{array}$

Problem Solving ■ Application

16 There are 365 days in one year. How many days are in two years?

_____________ days

HOME ACTIVITY • Make up some 3-digit story problems for your child to solve.

Name ______________________________

More 3-Digit Addition

There are 365 books about polar bears and 208 books about penguins. How many books are there altogether?

Step 1

Add the ones. Regroup if you need to. Write the number of ones.

$$\begin{array}{r} {}^{1} \\ 365 \\ +208 \\ \hline 3 \end{array}$$

Step 2

Add the tens. Regroup if you need to. Write the number of tens.

$$\begin{array}{r} {}^{1} \\ 365 \\ +208 \\ \hline 73 \end{array}$$

Step 3

Add the hundreds. Write the number of hundreds.

$$\begin{array}{r} {}^{1} \\ 365 \\ +208 \\ \hline 573 \end{array}$$

There are __573__ books altogether.

Add.

1. $\begin{array}{r} {}^{1} \\ 522 \\ +185 \\ \hline 707 \end{array}$

2. $\begin{array}{r} 907 \\ +\ \ 30 \\ \hline \end{array}$

3. $\begin{array}{r} 226 \\ +457 \\ \hline \end{array}$

4. $\begin{array}{r} 544 \\ +315 \\ \hline \end{array}$

5. $\begin{array}{r} 248 \\ +537 \\ \hline \end{array}$

6. $\begin{array}{r} 653 \\ +\ \ 37 \\ \hline \end{array}$

7. $\begin{array}{r} 193 \\ +284 \\ \hline \end{array}$

8. $\begin{array}{r} 25 \\ +492 \\ \hline \end{array}$

9. $\begin{array}{r} 709 \\ +259 \\ \hline \end{array}$

10. $\begin{array}{r} 888 \\ +\ \ \ 9 \\ \hline \end{array}$

11. $\begin{array}{r} 282 \\ +254 \\ \hline \end{array}$

12. $\begin{array}{r} 303 \\ +353 \\ \hline \end{array}$

Talk About It ■ **Reasoning**

Why do you regroup the ones if the sum is ten or more?

Add.

1 853 + 72 = 925	**2** 690 + 309	**3** 418 + 479	**4** 184 + 713
5 537 + 248	**6** 435 + 94	**7** 66 + 682	**8** 373 + 107
9 255 + 219	**10** 363 + 561	**11** 978 + 6	**12** 230 + 435
13 772 + 47	**14** 431 + 322	**15** 83 + 385	**16** 151 + 444

Mixed Review

Add or subtract.

17

45 + 35	65 − 16	94 − 53	73¢ − 29¢	82 + 4	24 + 58

HOME ACTIVITY • Using a book that has 500 or fewer pages, pick any two pages and point out the page numbers. Ask your child to add the two numbers on a sheet of paper. Repeat with other numbers.

Name ______________________________

Add Money

Sara bought a birdcage for $4.80 and a bird swing for $3.65. How much did she spend altogether?

$$\begin{array}{r} \$4.80 \\ +\$3.65 \\ \hline \$8.45 \end{array}$$

She spent $8.45 altogether.

Add money amounts the same way you add other numbers. Place a dollar sign and a decimal point in the sum.

decimal point → $4.80
dollar sign → $4.80

$$\begin{array}{r} \$4.80 \\ +\$3.65 \\ \hline \end{array}$$

Add.

1 $\begin{array}{r} \$1.22 \\ +\$5.58 \\ \hline \$6.80 \end{array}$	**2** $\begin{array}{r} \$5.71 \\ +\$4.13 \\ \hline \end{array}$	**3** $\begin{array}{r} \$6.18 \\ +\$1.43 \\ \hline \end{array}$	**4** $\begin{array}{r} \$4.18 \\ +\$0.90 \\ \hline \end{array}$
5 $\begin{array}{r} \$3.33 \\ +\$2.49 \\ \hline \end{array}$	**6** $\begin{array}{r} \$7.00 \\ +\$0.41 \\ \hline \end{array}$	**7** $\begin{array}{r} \$3.46 \\ +\$3.87 \\ \hline \end{array}$	**8** $\begin{array}{r} \$1.95 \\ +\$1.50 \\ \hline \end{array}$
9 $\begin{array}{r} \$1.37 \\ +\$5.50 \\ \hline \end{array}$	**10** $\begin{array}{r} \$7.34 \\ +\$1.44 \\ \hline \end{array}$	**11** $\begin{array}{r} \$2.09 \\ +\$1.13 \\ \hline \end{array}$	**12** $\begin{array}{r} \$3.95 \\ +\$3.00 \\ \hline \end{array}$

Talk About It ■ Reasoning

Tony has 2 dollar bills and 3 quarters in his wallet. Sarah has 275 pennies in her bank. Each thinks he or she has the most money. What do you think?

Add.

1 $2.62 + $3.84 = $6.46	**2** $5.25 + $3.90	**3** $0.55 + $6.29	**4** $2.44 + $7.37
5 $1.31 + $3.64	**6** $1.50 + $4.99	**7** $3.08 + $3.56	**8** $0.29 + $4.50
9 $3.33 + $5.53	**10** $3.57 + $1.28	**11** $2.16 + $3.45	**12** $7.50 + $2.40
13 $4.00 + $5.25	**14** $7.40 + $0.99	**15** $0.09 + $6.48	**16** $2.25 + $2.83

Problem Solving ■ Estimation

Estimate.

17 You want to buy a fish tank for $4.99 and a goldfish for $1.75. About how much money will you spend in all?

about ________

HOME ACTIVITY • Look in the newspaper for sale pages. Have your child pick any two prices under $5.00 and add the two amounts on a sheet of paper. Repeat several times.

Name ______________________________

UNDERSTAND › PLAN › SOLVE › CHECK

Choose a method to solve the problem.

472 + 407 = __?__

	You can use paper and pencil.	You can use a calculator.
What is 479 + 400? Say 479. Count on by hundreds. **479** 579, 679, 779, 879 479 + 400 = 879		

Choose a method to solve each problem.

1 $\begin{array}{r} 482 \\ +\ \ 26 \\ \hline 508 \end{array}$	**2** $\begin{array}{r} 430 \\ +306 \\ \hline \end{array}$	**3** $\begin{array}{r} \$0.25 \\ +\$5.47 \\ \hline \end{array}$	**4** $\begin{array}{r} 264 \\ +700 \\ \hline \end{array}$
5 $\begin{array}{r} 547 \\ +300 \\ \hline \end{array}$	**6** $\begin{array}{r} 85 \\ +483 \\ \hline \end{array}$	**7** $\begin{array}{r} 562 \\ +\ \ 10 \\ \hline \end{array}$	**8** $\begin{array}{r} 291 \\ +143 \\ \hline \end{array}$
9 $\begin{array}{r} 208 \\ +\ \ \ 1 \\ \hline \end{array}$	**10** $\begin{array}{r} \$0.75 \\ +\$3.90 \\ \hline \end{array}$	**11** $\begin{array}{r} 240 \\ +\ \ \ 3 \\ \hline \end{array}$	**12** $\begin{array}{r} \$7.67 \\ +\$1.00 \\ \hline \end{array}$

Choose a method to solve each problem. Rewrite the numbers in each problem. Then add.

You can use mental math.	You can use paper and pencil.	You can use a calculator.
Count on ones, tens, hundreds.		

1. 275 + 392

$$\begin{array}{r} 275 \\ +392 \\ \hline 667 \end{array}$$

2. 547 + 300

3. 27 + 608

4. 236 + 100

5. 151 + 393

6. 175 + 20

Problem Solving ■ Mental Math

Add.

7.

Add 100.	
108	208
256	
696	
847	

8.

Add 300.	
45	345
177	
284	
678	

9.

Add 500.	
89	589
205	
386	
440	

HOME ACTIVITY • Have your child tell you how to add 3-digit numbers. Together, make up addition problems using the digits from your phone number. The sums should be 999 or less.

Name ______________________________

CHECK ■ Concepts and Skills

Add.

1

$$\begin{array}{r} 1 \\ +7 \\ \hline \end{array} \qquad \begin{array}{r} 1 \text{ hundred} \\ +7 \text{ hundreds} \\ \hline \text{hundreds} \end{array} \qquad \begin{array}{r} 100 \\ +700 \\ \hline \end{array}$$

2

$$\begin{array}{r} 3 \\ +3 \\ \hline \end{array} \qquad \begin{array}{r} 3 \text{ hundreds} \\ +3 \text{ hundreds} \\ \hline \text{hundreds} \end{array} \qquad \begin{array}{r} 300 \\ +300 \\ \hline \end{array}$$

Use ▦ ▭ ▪. Add. Regroup if you need to.

3

hundreds	tens	ones
□	□	
6	1	8
+ 2	7	4

4

hundreds	tens	ones
□	□	
1	2	0
+ 3	3	8

5

hundreds	tens	ones
□	□	
3	8	3
+ 4	4	6

Add.

6

hundreds	tens	ones
□	□	
8	1	9
+	7	6

7

hundreds	tens	ones
□	□	
1	3	7
+ 6	0	0

8

hundreds	tens	ones
□	□	
4	5	2
+ 4	9	0

CHECK ■ Problem Solving

Choose a method to solve each problem.

9

$$\begin{array}{r} \$8.08 \\ +\$1.70 \\ \hline \end{array}$$

10

$$\begin{array}{r} 859 \\ +\quad 2 \\ \hline \end{array}$$

11

$$\begin{array}{r} \$2.17 \\ +\$3.00 \\ \hline \end{array}$$

12

$$\begin{array}{r} 55 \\ +574 \\ \hline \end{array}$$

Name ______________________________

Choose the best answer for questions 1–6.

1

$$\begin{array}{r} 200 \\ +\ 700 \\ \hline \end{array}$$

9 ○ 90 ○ 99 ○ 900 ○

2

$$\begin{array}{r} 434 \\ +\ 512 \\ \hline \end{array}$$

922 ○ 940 ○ 946 ○ 948 ○

3

$$\begin{array}{r} \$1.85 \\ +\ \$5.12 \\ \hline \end{array}$$

$4.73 ○ $6.73 ○ $6.97 ○ $7.97 ○

4

$$\begin{array}{r} 703 \\ +\ 105 \\ \hline \end{array}$$

602 ○ 608 ○ 802 ○ 808 ○

5

$$\begin{array}{r} \$4.56 \\ +\ \$3.22 \\ \hline \end{array}$$

$7.78 ○ $7.84 ○

$8.84 ○ $17.84 ○

6 Michael has 2 football cards and 4 baseball cards. What fraction of the group is football cards?

$\frac{2}{4}$ ○ $\frac{2}{6}$ ○ $\frac{4}{6}$ ○ $\frac{6}{6}$ ○

Show What You Know

7 Use . Make up your own addition problems. Write the numbers.

Regroup once.

hundreds	tens	ones
□	□	
+		
5	7	1

Regroup twice.

hundreds	tens	ones
□	□	
+		
6	3	2

CHAPTER 26

Subtracting 3-Digit Numbers

Write as many subtraction problems as you can, using the numbers in the picture.

School-Home Connection

Dear Family,

Today we started Chapter 26. We will look at ways to subtract 3-digit numbers. Here is the math vocabulary and an activity for us to do together at home.

Love,

____

My Math Word

regroup

Vocabulary

regroup To break 1 hundred into 10 tens or to break 1 ten into 10 ones.

$$\begin{array}{r} {\scriptstyle 7\ 14} \\ \not{8}\not{4}5 \\ -\ 375 \\ \hline 470 \end{array}$$

Regroup 1 hundred as 10 tens. Then you have 7 hundreds and 14 tens.

Activity

Before you take a trip, discuss the total number of miles you will travel. Then along the way, look at road signs that give the distance in miles to your destination. Ask your child to subtract that distance from the total miles to find out how many miles you have traveled so far.

Books to Share

To read about 3-digit subtraction with your child, look for these books at your local library.

The King's Commissioners, by Aileen Friedman, Scholastic, 1995.

The Hundred Dresses, by Eleanor Estes, Harcourt, 1974.

The Philharmonic Gets Dressed, by Karla Kuskin, HarperCollins, 1986.

Visit *The Learning Site* for additional ideas and activities. www.harcourtschool.com

Name ______________________________

Subtract Hundreds

What is 500 − 300?

5 − 3 = 2

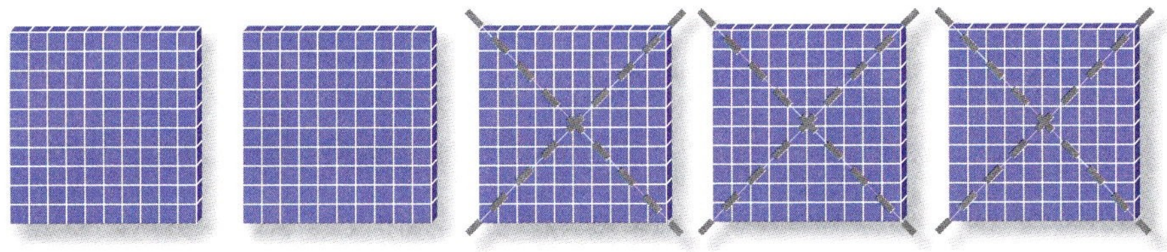

5 hundreds − 3 hundreds = 2 hundreds

500 − 300 = 200

Subtract.

1. 9 − 5 = ______

   9 hundreds − 5 hundreds = ______ hundreds

   900 − 500 = ______

---

2. 7 − 6 = ______

   7 hundreds − 6 hundreds = ______ hundreds

   700 − 600 = ______

---

3. 8 − 5 = ______

   8 hundreds − 5 hundreds = ______ hundreds

   800 − 500 = ______

Talk About It ▪ **Reasoning**

How does knowing 6 − 3 help you find 600 − 300? Explain your thinking.

Subtract.

1. 4 − 1 = 3 | 4 hundreds − 1 hundred = 3 hundreds | 400 − 100 = 300

2. 7 − 3 = ___ | 7 hundreds − 3 hundreds = ___ hundreds | 700 − 300 = ___

3. 9 − 7 = ___ | 9 hundreds − 7 hundreds = ___ hundreds | 900 − 700 = ___

4. 8 − 4 = ___ | 8 hundreds − 4 hundreds = ___ hundreds | 800 − 400 = ___

5. 5 − 4 = ___ | 5 hundreds − 4 hundreds = ___ hundred | 500 − 400 = ___

6. 8 − 6 = ___ | 8 hundreds − 6 hundreds = ___ hundreds | 800 − 600 = ___

7. 4 − 4 = ___ | 4 hundreds − 4 hundreds = ___ hundreds | 400 − 400 = ___

8. 9 − 6 = ___ | 9 hundreds − 6 hundreds = ___ hundreds | 900 − 600 = ___

Algebra

Use addition to subtract.

9. 500 + 300 = 800, so 800 − ______ = 500

10. 200 + 700 = 900, so 900 − ______ = 200

11. 400 + 300 = 700, so 700 − ______ = 400

HOME ACTIVITY • Put out 5 dollars and take away 1. Remind your child that each dollar is worth 100 cents. Ask your child to find 5 − 1 (4) and then 500 − 100 (400). Repeat with other groups of dollars.

Name ____________________

Model 3-Digit Subtraction

236 − 129 = ____

Step 1
Show 236.
Look at the ones.
Should you regroup?

Yes (circled)   No

hundreds	tens	ones
	☐	☐
2	3	6
− 1	2	9

Step 2
Regroup 1 ten as 10 ones. Now there are 16 ones. Subtract 9 from 16.
Write how many ones are left.

hundreds	tens	ones
	2	16
2	~~3~~	~~6~~
− 1	2	9
		7

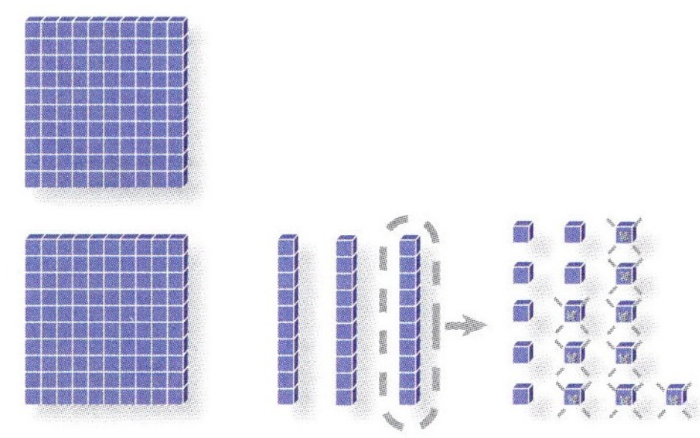

Step 3
Subtract the tens.
Subtract the hundreds.
Write how many tens and hundreds are left.

hundreds	tens	ones
	2	16
2	~~3~~	~~6~~
− 1	2	9
1	0	7

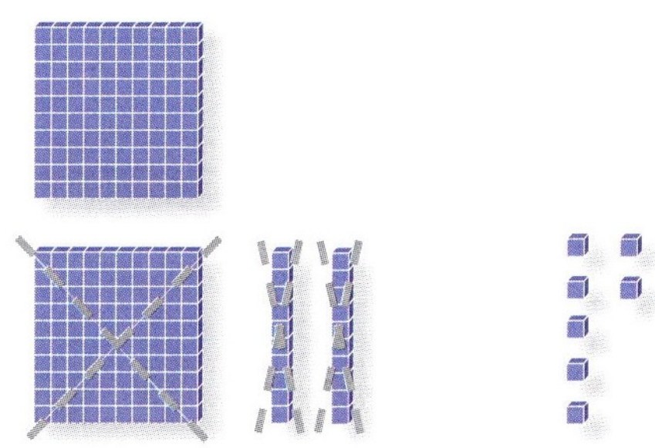

Use hundreds, tens, ones blocks. Subtract.

1

hundreds	tens	ones
	☐	☐
9	6	3
− 7	5	7

2

hundreds	tens	ones
	☐	☐
7	8	7
− 2	4	5

3

hundreds	tens	ones
	☐	☐
6	4	1
− 3	2	5

Talk About It ■ **Reasoning**

Why is it easier to subtract ones first?

Use hundreds, tens, ones blocks. Subtract.

1

	hundreds	tens	ones
		4	10
	8	5	0
−	6	1	3
	2	3	7

2

	hundreds	tens	ones
		☐	☐
	9	8	2
−	9	1	9

3

	hundreds	tens	ones
		☐	☐
	5	9	0
−	2	3	8

4

	hundreds	tens	ones
		☐	☐
	4	2	8
−	1	1	3

5

	hundreds	tens	ones
		☐	☐
	7	9	4
−	2	5	7

6

	hundreds	tens	ones
		☐	☐
	6	4	8
−		3	9

7

	hundreds	tens	ones
		☐	☐
	3	9	1
−	1	0	6

8

	hundreds	tens	ones
		☐	☐
	8	6	5
−		3	8

9

	hundreds	tens	ones
		☐	☐
	7	7	5
−	6	0	7

Problem Solving ■ Mental Math

Count on to add. Count back to subtract.

10 $428 + 30 =$ _____

11 $157 + 300 =$ _____

12 $563 - 100 =$ _____

13 $296 - 20 =$ _____

HOME ACTIVITY • Have your child choose a subtraction problem on this page and tell you the steps he or she followed to solve it.

Name ______________________

Subtract 3-Digit Numbers

329 − 197 = ____

Step 1

Show 329.
Subtract the ones.
Write how many ones are left.

hundreds	tens	ones
☐	☐	
3	2	9
− 1	9	7
		2

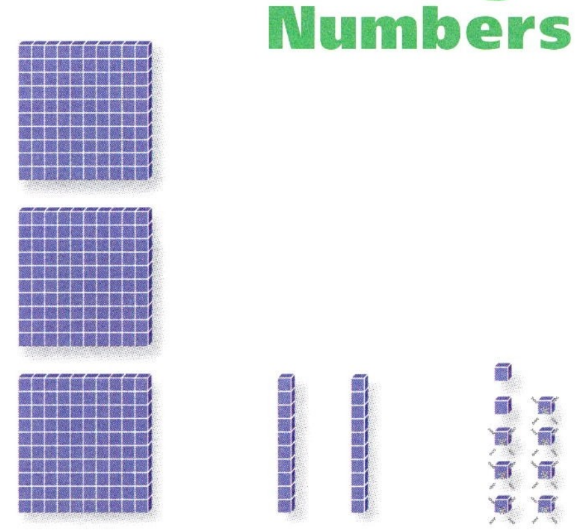

Step 2

Can you subtract 9 tens? If not, regroup 1 hundred as 10 tens. Now there are 12 tens. Subtract. Write how many tens are left.

hundreds	tens	ones
2	12	
~~3~~	~~2~~	9
− 1	9	7
	3	2

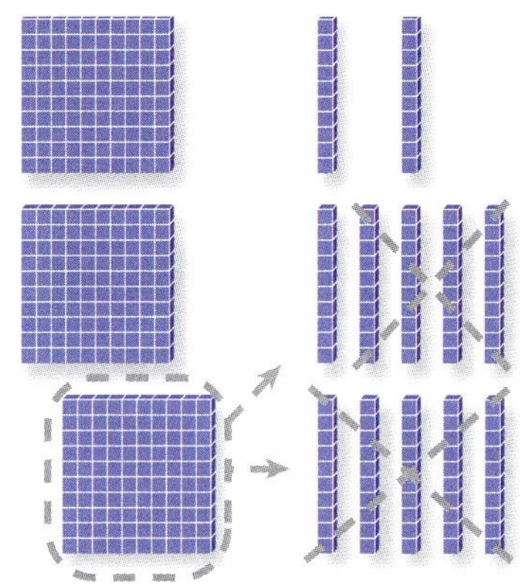

Step 3

Subtract the hundreds.
Write how many hundreds are left.

hundreds	tens	ones
2	12	
3	~~2~~	9
− 1	9	7
1	3	2

Subtract.

1

hundreds	tens	ones
☐	☐	
8	4	8
− 4	7	5

2

hundreds	tens	ones
☐	☐	
9	2	4
− 6	5	3

3

hundreds	tens	ones
☐	☐	
7	5	9
− 1	9	5

Talk About It ■ **Reasoning**

What happens if you subtract the hundreds first when you subtract 3-digit numbers?

Subtract.

1

hundreds	tens	ones
6	10	
~~7~~	~~0~~	7
− 1	6	3
5	4	4

2

hundreds	tens	ones
☐	☐	
9	4	6
− 5	8	3

3

hundreds	tens	ones
	☐	☐
3	8	1
−	4	4

4

hundreds	tens	ones
☐	☐	
8	2	8
− 6	7	4

5

hundreds	tens	ones
☐	☐	
5	2	7
− 2	4	5

6

hundreds	tens	ones
	☐	☐
8	4	2
− 3	2	6

7

hundreds	tens	ones
☐	☐	
6	0	4
− 3	1	0

8

hundreds	tens	ones
	☐	☐
9	8	7
− 1	6	9

9

hundreds	tens	ones
	☐	☐
7	3	6
− 7	1	7

Mixed Review

Find the pattern. Write the rule. Continue the pattern.

10 Edie sees a pattern in the numbers 819, 719, 619.

The rule could be count ______________________.

819, 719, 619, ______, ______, ______, ______, ______

HOME ACTIVITY • Give your child two 3-digit numbers and have him or her subtract.

Name ______________________________

More 3-Digit Subtraction

There are 340 people at the beach.
137 of the people go in the water.
How many people do not go in the water?

Step 1
There are not enough ones to subtract without regrouping. Regroup 1 ten as 10 ones.

$$\begin{array}{r} \scriptstyle 3\,10 \\ 3\not{4}\not{0} \\ -\,137 \\ \hline \end{array}$$

Step 2
Subtract the ones.
Subtract the tens.

$$\begin{array}{r} \scriptstyle 3\,10 \\ 3\not{4}\not{0} \\ -\,137 \\ \hline 03 \end{array}$$

Step 3
Subtract the hundreds.

$$\begin{array}{r} \scriptstyle 3\,10 \\ 3\not{4}\not{0} \\ -\,137 \\ \hline 203 \end{array}$$

203 people do not go in the water.

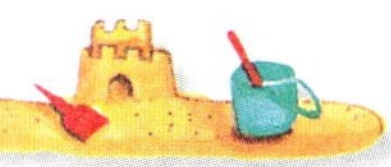

Subtract.

1 $\begin{array}{r} \scriptstyle 8\,12 \\ \not{9}\not{2}6 \\ -\;45 \\ \hline 881 \end{array}$	**2** $\begin{array}{r} 739 \\ -284 \\ \hline \end{array}$	**3** $\begin{array}{r} 409 \\ -206 \\ \hline \end{array}$	**4** $\begin{array}{r} 198 \\ -\;48 \\ \hline \end{array}$
5 $\begin{array}{r} 542 \\ -226 \\ \hline \end{array}$	**6** $\begin{array}{r} 673 \\ -\;37 \\ \hline \end{array}$	**7** $\begin{array}{r} 603 \\ -353 \\ \hline \end{array}$	**8** $\begin{array}{r} 258 \\ -142 \\ \hline \end{array}$
9 $\begin{array}{r} 709 \\ -259 \\ \hline \end{array}$	**10** $\begin{array}{r} 888 \\ -\;9 \\ \hline \end{array}$	**11** $\begin{array}{r} 532 \\ -250 \\ \hline \end{array}$	**12** $\begin{array}{r} 190 \\ -\;84 \\ \hline \end{array}$

Talk About It ▪ **Reasoning**
How do you know if you need to regroup? Explain with examples.

Subtract.

1. $\begin{array}{r} \scriptstyle 4\,10 \\ 506 \\ -\ 452 \\ \hline 54 \end{array}$	2. $\begin{array}{r} 675 \\ -\ 94 \\ \hline \end{array}$	3. $\begin{array}{r} 864 \\ -\ 123 \\ \hline \end{array}$	4. $\begin{array}{r} 458 \\ -\ 29 \\ \hline \end{array}$
5. $\begin{array}{r} 903 \\ -\ 250 \\ \hline \end{array}$	6. $\begin{array}{r} 784 \\ -\ 7 \\ \hline \end{array}$	7. $\begin{array}{r} 965 \\ -\ 781 \\ \hline \end{array}$	8. $\begin{array}{r} 175 \\ -\ 57 \\ \hline \end{array}$
9. $\begin{array}{r} 688 \\ -\ 347 \\ \hline \end{array}$	10. $\begin{array}{r} 393 \\ -\ 78 \\ \hline \end{array}$	11. $\begin{array}{r} 950 \\ -\ 370 \\ \hline \end{array}$	12. $\begin{array}{r} 566 \\ -\ 425 \\ \hline \end{array}$
13. $\begin{array}{r} 837 \\ -\ 263 \\ \hline \end{array}$	14. $\begin{array}{r} 698 \\ -\ 68 \\ \hline \end{array}$	15. $\begin{array}{r} 759 \\ -\ 555 \\ \hline \end{array}$	16. $\begin{array}{r} 390 \\ -\ 147 \\ \hline \end{array}$

Problem Solving ■ Reasoning

Write the two numbers that make each difference. Use the numbers in the box.

897	653
543	252

17. Difference of 645 ______ and ______

18. Difference of 110 ______ and ______

HOME ACTIVITY • Make up a subtraction problem using two 3-digit numbers. Ask your child to find the difference on a sheet of paper. Repeat with other problems.

Name ____________________

UNDERSTAND › PLAN › SOLVE › CHECK

Draw a line through the sentence that is not needed. Then solve.

1 While on a trip, the Rodriguez family sees 156 trucks and 138 vans. ~~They see 65 station wagons.~~ How many more trucks than vans do they see?

18 more trucks.

$$\begin{array}{r} \scriptstyle 4\,16 \\ 1\,5\,6 \\ -\ 1\,3\,8 \\ \hline 1\,8 \end{array}$$

2 They drive 507 miles on Monday. They drive 245 miles on Tuesday. They drive 428 miles on Wednesday. How many more miles do they drive on Monday than on Tuesday?

_______ more miles.

3 Mr. Rodriguez buys juice for $2.25. Juan buys snacks for $1.49. Juan gets trail mix. How much money do they spend altogether?

____

4 Susie has 140 postcards. The postcards cost 18¢ each. She sends 32 postcards. How many postcards does Susie have left?

_______ postcards

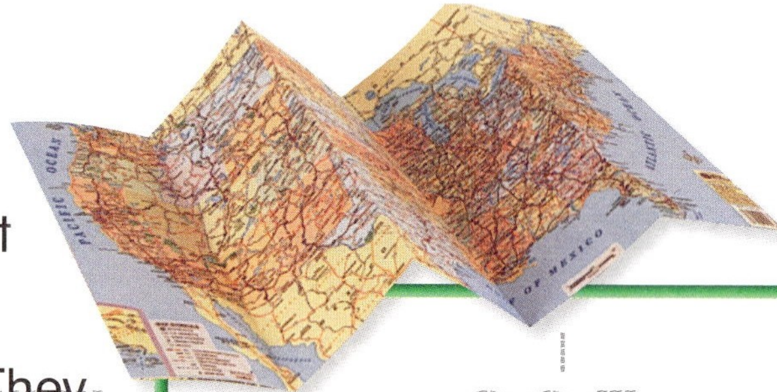

Draw a line through the sentence that is not needed. Then solve.

1. Mr. Rodriguez drives 335 miles. ~~They stop to eat lunch for 1 hour.~~ Then they drive 238 miles more. How many miles do they drive in all?

573 miles

$$\begin{array}{r} 335 \\ +\,238 \\ \hline 573 \end{array}$$

2. Juan counts 235 cars. Susie counts 247 cars. Mrs. Rodriguez counts 303 cars. How many fewer cars does Juan count than Suzie?

_______ fewer cars

3. Nevada Falls is 594 feet high. Smith Falls is 320 feet high. It is 100 feet wide at the top. How much higher is Nevada Falls than Smith Falls?

_______ feet

4. The family hikes on a trail for 5 hours. They see 125 sparrows. They see 165 ravens. How many sparrows and ravens do they see altogether?

_______ sparrows and ravens

Math Journal

Write About It

Write a word problem for a classmate to solve.
Put in one sentence that is not needed to solve the problem.

HOME ACTIVITY • **Have your child explain to you how he or she solved the problems in this lesson.**

Name ______________________________

CHECK ▪ Concepts and Skills

Subtract.

1

9	9 hundreds	900
− 6	− 6 hundreds	− 600
___	___ hundreds	___

2

5	5 hundreds	500
− 3	− 3 hundreds	− 300
___	___ hundreds	___

Use 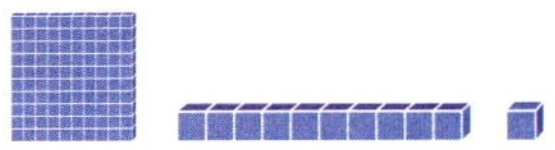 . Subtract.

3

hundreds	tens	ones
☐	☐	☐
7	1	8
− 4	4	5

4

hundreds	tens	ones
☐	☐	☐
4	6	9
− 3	7	2

5

hundreds	tens	ones
☐	☐	☐
5	5	0
−	2	4

Subtract.

6 $\begin{array}{r} 633 \\ -170 \\ \hline \end{array}$

7 $\begin{array}{r} 743 \\ -\ 26 \\ \hline \end{array}$

8 $\begin{array}{r} 956 \\ -592 \\ \hline \end{array}$

9 $\begin{array}{r} 244 \\ -226 \\ \hline \end{array}$

CHECK ▪ Problem Solving

Draw a line through the sentence that is not needed. Then solve.

10 Dad has a beehive with 634 bees. He gets a new hive with 529 bees. The bees make 60 pounds of honey. How many fewer bees are in the new hive?

_______ fewer bees

Name ______________________

Choose the best answer for questions 1–7.

1

$$\begin{array}{r} 800 \\ -\ 600 \\ \hline \end{array}$$

2 ○ 200 ○ 300 ○ 2000 ○

2

$$\begin{array}{r} 726 \\ -\ 302 \\ \hline \end{array}$$

416 ○ 424 ○ 428 ○ 1028 ○

3

$$\begin{array}{r} 532 \\ -\ 520 \\ \hline \end{array}$$

6 ○ 11 ○ 12 ○ 46 ○

4

$$\begin{array}{r} 356 \\ -\ 145 \\ \hline \end{array}$$

211 ○ 389 ○ 400 ○ 401 ○

5

$$\begin{array}{r} \$4.56 \\ +\ \$3.48 \\ \hline \end{array}$$

$1.08 ○ $1.09 ○ $8.09 ○ $8.04 ○

6 What number is just after 326?

327 ○ 328 ○ 427 ○ 527 ○

7 Together, Matt and Ann have 145 stickers. 23 of the stickers have flowers. 45 of the stickers belong to Matt. How many belong to Ann?

100 ○ 213 ○ 190 ○ 290 ○

Show What You Know

8 Use 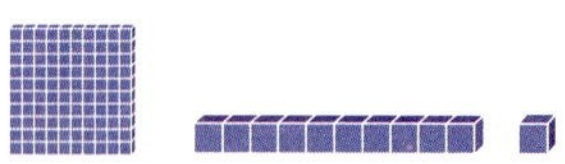. Make up your own subtraction problems. Write the numbers.

Regroup once.

hundreds	tens	ones
□	□	
–		
2	4	8

Regroup twice.

hundreds	tens	ones
□	□	□
–		
1	8	7

CHAPTER 27

Use Addition and Subtraction

You can buy 3 toys. About how much money will you need?

© Harcourt

SCHOOL HOME CONNECTION

Dear Family,

Today we started Chapter 27. We will use addition and subtraction of 3-digit numbers in new ways. Here is the math vocabulary and an activity for us to do together at home.

Love,

____

My Math Words

estimate sums
estimate differences

Vocabulary

estimate sums To find *about* how many in all. One way to do this is to round each number to the closer hundred and add the hundreds.

Estimate 179 is about 200; $+493$ is about $+500$; 700

$$\begin{array}{r} 179 \\ +493 \\ \hline \end{array} \text{ is about } \begin{array}{r} 200 \\ +500 \\ \hline 700 \end{array}$$

So, 179 + 493 is about 700.

estimate differences To find *about* how many are left. One way to do this is to round each number to the closer hundred and subtract the hundreds.

$$\begin{array}{r} 775 \\ -318 \\ \hline \end{array} \text{ is about } \begin{array}{r} 800 \\ -300 \\ \hline 500 \end{array}$$

So, 775 – 318 is about 500.

Visit *The Learning Site* for additional ideas and activities. www.harcourtschool.com

ACTIVITY

When shopping at the supermarket, help your child compare prices. Choose two similar items that weigh the same amount. The items should cost between $1.00 and $4.99. Have your child estimate the difference in price between the two items and tell which is the better buy.

Books to Share

To read about 3-digit addition and subtraction with your child, look for these books in your local library.

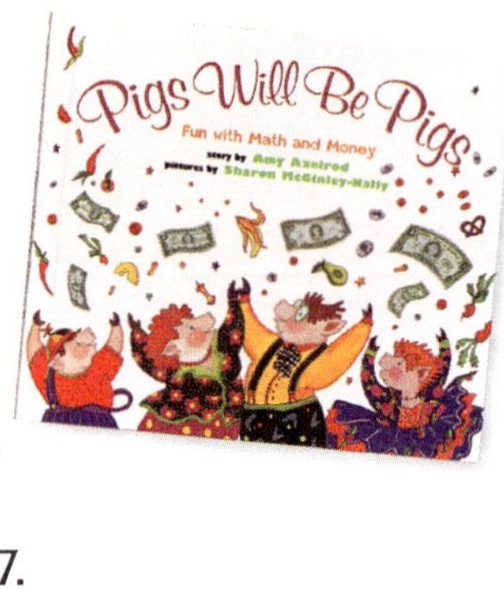

Pigs Will Be Pigs, by Amy Axelrod, Simon & Schuster, 1994.

Easy Math Puzzles, by David A. Adler, Holiday House, 1997.

Name ______________________________

Add and Subtract Money

Kareem took $7.45 to the pet store.
He bought a fish tank for $4.17.
How much money does he have left?

Read the decimal point as **and**. $1.20 can be read one dollar **and** twenty cents.

decimal point → .
dollar sign → $

$$\begin{array}{r} \$7.45 \\ -\$4.17 \\ \hline \end{array}$$

Step 1

Subtract the ones. Regroup if you need to. Write how many ones are left.

$$\begin{array}{r} {\scriptstyle 3\ 15} \\ \$7.\not{4}\not{5} \\ -\$4.17 \\ \hline 8 \end{array}$$

Step 2

Subtract the tens. Regroup if you need to. Write how many tens are left.

$$\begin{array}{r} {\scriptstyle 3\ 15} \\ \$7.\not{4}\not{5} \\ -\$4.17 \\ \hline 28 \end{array}$$

Step 3

Subtract the hundreds. Write how many are left. Write the dollar sign and the decimal point.

$$\begin{array}{r} {\scriptstyle 3\ 15} \\ \$7.\not{4}\not{5} \\ -\$4.17 \\ \hline \$3.28 \end{array}$$

He had $3.28 left.

Add or subtract.

1. $$\begin{array}{r} \$3.02 \\ +\$2.58 \\ \hline \end{array}$$
2. $$\begin{array}{r} \$5.52 \\ -\$5.28 \\ \hline \end{array}$$
3. $$\begin{array}{r} \$7.50 \\ +\$0.41 \\ \hline \end{array}$$
4. $$\begin{array}{r} \$8.69 \\ -\$3.87 \\ \hline \end{array}$$
5. $$\begin{array}{r} \$3.95 \\ +\$5.50 \\ \hline \end{array}$$
6. $$\begin{array}{r} \$9.99 \\ -\$8.45 \\ \hline \end{array}$$
7. $$\begin{array}{r} \$6.05 \\ -\$3.84 \\ \hline \end{array}$$
8. $$\begin{array}{r} \$4.25 \\ +\$1.35 \\ \hline \end{array}$$

Talk About It ■ **Reasoning**

How is subtracting dollars and cents the same as subtracting 3-digit numbers? How is it different?

Add or subtract.

Remember, write the dollar sign and decimal point in your answer.

1 $6.45 − $1.55 = $4.90	**2** $3.36 − $0.17	**3** $5.99 + $1.00	**4** $4.58 − $3.73
5 $2.95 + $6.72	**6** $5.86 − $3.45	**7** $6.05 − $3.84	**8** $4.56 + $4.36
9 $0.63 + $6.00	**10** $7.47 − $2.45	**11** $9.75 − $5.91	**12** $2.15 + $6.35
13 $8.46 − $4.08	**14** $2.37 − $1.53	**15** $7.39 + $1.66	**16** $4.58 − $3.39

Problem Solving ▪ Number Sense

Circle yes or no.

17 You want to buy a fish tank for $4.99. You have $5.00. Do you have enough money?

yes no

18 You have $1.00. You want to buy a turtle for $1.99. Do you have enough money?

yes no

HOME ACTIVITY • Look in the newspaper for sale pages. Have your child pick any two prices under $5.00 and add or subtract the two amounts. Repeat several times.

Name ______________________________

Estimate Sums and Differences

Tim wants a train that costs $3.98 and a ball that costs $2.95. About how much money does Tim need? First use rounding to estimate the sum. Then solve. Was your answer reasonable?

Estimate	Solve
$4.00 + $3.00 $7.00	$3.98 + $2.95 $6.93

For 50¢ or more, round to the next dollar.

$3.98 is about $4.00.
$2.95 is about $3.00.

$6.93 is about $7.00, so the answer is reasonable.

Round to estimate.
Then add or subtract to solve.

1 Ei has $8.72. Julia has $4.63. How much more money does Ei have than Julia?

____

Estimate	Solve

2 Lynnette has $2.89. She gets $2.80 more. How much money does she have altogether?

____

Estimate	Solve

Talk About It • Reasoning

Why might you estimate to add and subtract 3-digit numbers?

Round to estimate.
Then add or subtract to solve.

1. Tonio has $8.99.
Earl has $5.85.
How much more money does Tonio have than Earl?
$3.14

2. Tonio takes all of his money to the pet store. He buys a cat toy for $4.68. How much money does he have left?
______

3. Earl wants to buy cat food for $3.75 and a cat collar for $.98. How much money will he spend in all?
______

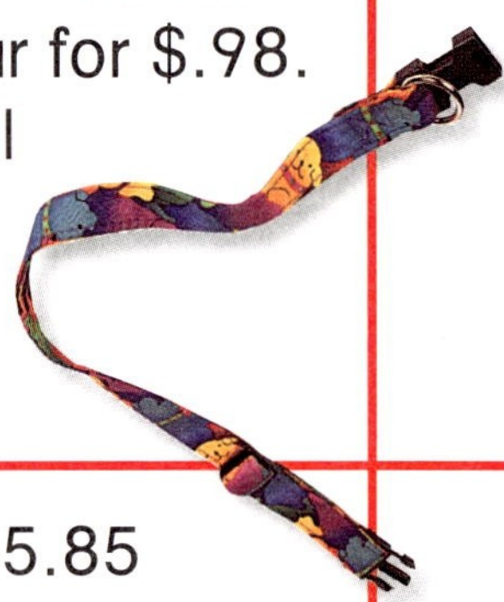

4. How much of Earl's $5.85 will he have left after he buys the cat food and the cat collar?
______

	Estimate	Solve
1	$9.00 − $6.00 $3.00	$8.99 − $5.85 $3.14
2		
3		
4		

Problem Solving ■ **Reasoning**

5. Janine wants a book for $2.49 and some markers for $1.25. She estimates she will need about $3.00. Is she correct? Why or why not?

HOME ACTIVITY • **Have your child tell you why he or she estimated the way he or she did on this page.**

Name ______________________________

Practice Adding and Subtracting 3-Digit Numbers

Add or subtract.

1
$$\begin{array}{r} \scriptstyle 5\,10 \\ 605 \\ -443 \\ \hline 162 \end{array}$$

2
$$\begin{array}{r} \$8.75 \\ -\$0.59 \\ \hline \end{array}$$

3
$$\begin{array}{r} 646 \\ +100 \\ \hline \end{array}$$

4
$$\begin{array}{r} 555 \\ -381 \\ \hline \end{array}$$

5
$$\begin{array}{r} \$5.45 \\ +\$4.25 \\ \hline \end{array}$$

6
$$\begin{array}{r} 752 \\ -339 \\ \hline \end{array}$$

7
$$\begin{array}{r} 685 \\ -302 \\ \hline \end{array}$$

8
$$\begin{array}{r} 467 \\ +450 \\ \hline \end{array}$$

9
$$\begin{array}{r} 63 \\ +631 \\ \hline \end{array}$$

10
$$\begin{array}{r} \$7.82 \\ -\$2.10 \\ \hline \end{array}$$

11
$$\begin{array}{r} 956 \\ -595 \\ \hline \end{array}$$

12
$$\begin{array}{r} \$1.57 \\ +\$4.23 \\ \hline \end{array}$$

13
$$\begin{array}{r} 469 \\ -408 \\ \hline \end{array}$$

14
$$\begin{array}{r} 333 \\ -153 \\ \hline \end{array}$$

15
$$\begin{array}{r} 846 \\ -839 \\ \hline \end{array}$$

16
$$\begin{array}{r} 675 \\ -564 \\ \hline \end{array}$$

Talk About It ■ Reasoning

How can estimating help you find out if your answer makes sense?

Add or subtract. Use the code to answer the riddle.

375 – 400: A	526 – 550: G	676 – 700: M	826 – 850: S
401 – 425: B	551 – 575: H	701 – 725: N	851 – 875: T
426 – 450: C	576 – 600: I	726 – 750: O	876 – 900: U
451 – 475: D	601 – 625: J	751 – 775: P	901 – 925: V
476 – 500: E	626 – 650: K	776 – 800: Q	926 – 950: W
501 – 525: F	651 – 675: L	801 – 825: R	976 – 999: Y

Why can't you feed a teddy bear?

400 + 23	988 − 503	342 + 84	781 − 400	899 − 23	325 + 524	250 + 250
423	485	____	____	____	____	____
B	E	____	____	____	____	____

608 − 10	473 + 396	425 + 425
____	____	____
____	____ ,	____

425 + 415	860 − 5	446 + 430	219 + 302	590 − 80	532 − 42	371 + 93
____	____	____	____	____	____	____
____	____	____	____	____	____	____ !

HOME ACTIVITY • You and your child can have fun using the code on this page. Make up addition and subtraction problems with answers that spell out "I love you." Have your child solve the problems, write the letters, and read the message.

Name ______________________________

UNDERSTAND > PLAN > SOLVE > CHECK

Mary has $6.50. She buys a sandwich for $2.35 and milk for $1.15. How much money does Mary have left?

Step 1	Step 2
Add the amounts Mary spent. $2.35 + $1.15 $3.50	Subtract the sum from the amount Mary had to start with. $6.50 − $3.50 $3.00

Mary has $3.00 left.

Add or subtract.
Do one step at a time.

Step 1	Step 2

1. Sho has 481 trading cards. He sells 218 of his cards. Then he buys 156 more. How many cards does Sho have now?

_______ cards

2. Liz has 222 stamps in one book and 349 stamps in another book. If she gives 107 stamps to a friend, how many stamps will she have left?

_______ stamps

3. Steve weighs 172 pounds. Jan weighs 65 pounds. The ramp they are standing on holds up to 350 pounds. How many more pounds can the ramp hold?

_______ pounds

Add or subtract.
Do one step at a time.

1. The school has 755 books to sell. First grade sells 380 books. Second grade sells 259 books. How many books are left?

   116 books

2. Steve has saved 115 pennies. He gives 65 to his little sister. Steve saves 132 more pennies. Now how many pennies does Steve have?

   _______ pennies

3. Jenny has \$8.48 in her bank. She takes out \$2.45. Then she takes out \$6.00 more. How much money is left in the bank?

   ____

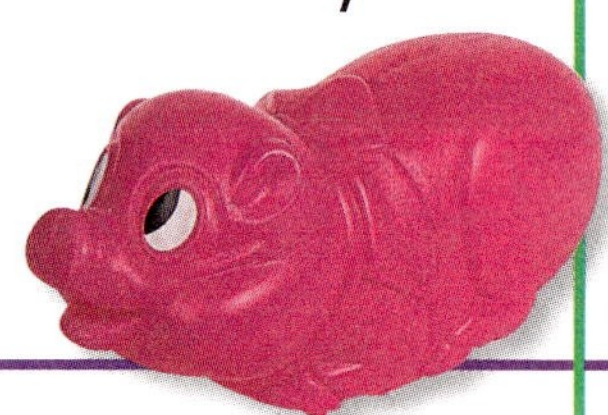

4. Greg has 309 blue blocks and 483 red blocks in a box. He uses 287 blocks for a building. How many blocks are still in the box?

   _______ blocks

	Step 1	Step 2
1	$\begin{array}{r} ^{1} \\ 380 \\ +259 \\ \hline 639 \end{array}$	$\begin{array}{r} ^{4\ 15} \\ 755 \\ -639 \\ \hline 116 \end{array}$
2		
3		
4		

Math Journal

Write About It

Make up your own multiple step problem.
Ask a friend to solve it.

HOME ACTIVITY • Together with your child, look at the exercises in this lesson. Ask your child to explain how he or she decided when to add or subtract. There may be more than one way to solve the problems.

Name ______________________

CHECK ■ Concepts and Skills

Add or subtract.

1. $6.60 − $3.57

2. $5.95 + $0.24

3. $9.48 − $2.15

4. $7.46 − $1.74

Round to estimate.
Then add or subtract to solve.

5. Edie has $3.80 in her bank. She gets $4.75 for her birthday. How much money does Edie have now?

______

Estimate	Solve

Add or subtract.

6. 112 + 549

7. $4.86 − $2.01

8. 762 + 42

9. 955 − 595

CHECK ■ Problem Solving

Add or subtract.
Do one step at a time.

10. Harry has $8.57. He buys a toy for $4.00. Then his grandpa gives him $2.25. How much money does Harry have now?

______

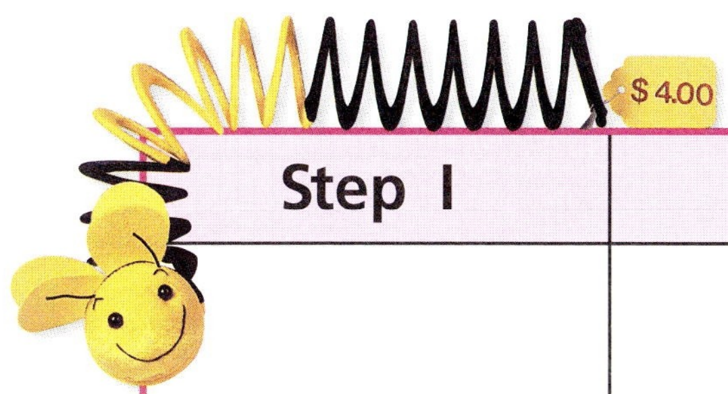

Step 1	Step 2

Name ______________________________

Choose the best answer for questions 1–5.

1

$$\begin{array}{r} 561 \\ +\ 238 \\ \hline \end{array}$$

231 ○ 337 ○ 798 ○ 799 ○

2

$$\begin{array}{r} 987 \\ -\ 659 \\ \hline \end{array}$$

228 ○ 328 ○ 329 ○ 332 ○

3 André has $7.23. Amy has $8.93. About how much more money does Amy have than André?

About $1.50 ○ About $2.00 ○ About $15.96 ○ About $16.00 ○

4 Which number tells how many?

13 ○ 147 ○ 148 ○ 418 ○

5 Demario had 275 basketball cards. He gave 98 of the cards to James. Then Demario got 104 more basketball cards. How many basketball cards did he have then?

171 ○ 177 ○ 281 ○ 477 ○

Show What You Know

6 Write a price between $2.00 and $3.00 on each tag. Find the cost of both toys together. Write the addition problem.

$.

\+ $.

$.

CHAPTER 28

Multiplication Concepts

SCHOOL HOME CONNECTION

Dear Family,

Today we started Chapter 28. We will learn how to multiply. Here is the math vocabulary and an activity for us to do together at home.

Love,

____

My Math Words

multiplication sentence

product

Vocabulary

multiplication sentence A number sentence that gives the total for a number of equal groups and the number in each group.

$5 \times 10 = 50$ is a multiplication sentence.

product The answer in a multiplication problem.

$4 \times 5 = 20$

↑ product

ACTIVITY

With your child, look for equal groups of 2, 3, 4, and 5. Groups of 2 and 4 might be the ears and legs on neighborhood animals. Groups of 3 and 5 might be flowers in a garden. Have your child draw pictures of the groups and write multiplication sentences to tell about the pictures.

Books to Share

To read about multiplication with your child, look for these books in your local library.

Each Orange Had 8 Slices,
by Paul Giganti, Jr.,
Greenwillow, 1992.

Amanda Bean's Amazing Dream,
by Cindy Neuschwander,
Scholastic, 1998.

Visit *The Learning Site* for additional ideas and activities. www.harcourtschool.com

Name ________________________________

Explore Multiplication

There are 5 **equal groups**.

There are 5 ■ in each group.

How many ■ are there in all?

5, 10, 15, 20, 25

There are 25 in all.

Make equal groups of ■.
Skip-count. Write how many in all.

1. Make 5 equal groups.
   Put 4 ■ in each group.

   ______, ______, ______, ______, ______ ______ in all

2. Make 4 equal groups.
   Put 10 ■ in each group.

   ______, ______, ______, ______ ______ in all

3. Make 5 equal groups.
   Put 3 ■ in each group.

   ______, ______, ______, ______, ______ ______ in all

4. Make 3 equal groups.
   Put 5 ■ in each group.

   ______, ______, ______ ______ in all

Talk About It ■ **Reasoning**

Why do you need equal groups to skip-count?

Make equal groups of ■.
Skip-count. Write how many in all.

1. Make 8 equal groups.
Put 10 ■ in each group.

10, 20, 30, ____, ____, ____, ____, ____

____ in all

2. Make 6 equal groups.
Put 2 ■ in each group.

____, ____, ____, ____, ____, ____ ____ in all

3. Make 5 equal groups.
Put 2 ■ in each group.

____, ____, ____, ____, ____ ____ in all

4. Make 7 equal groups.
Put 4 ■ in each group.

____, ____, ____, ____, ____, ____, ____

____ in all

Problem Solving ■ Number Sense

Does the answer make sense?
Circle yes or no.

5. There are 9 equal groups.
There are 3 in each group.
There are 135 in all.
yes no

6. There are 4 equal groups.
There are 10 in each group.
There are 14 in all.
yes no

HOME ACTIVITY • Make equal groups of pennies. Help your child find the total by skip-counting by the number of pennies in each group. Repeat, using a different number of pennies in the groups.

Name ______________________________

Addition and Multiplication

3 groups

Add.
$2 + 2 + 2 = 6$
The answer is called the sum.

Multiply.
$3 \times 2 = 6$
The answer is called the **product**.

$2 + 2 + 2 =$ 6

$3 \times 2 =$ 6

Write the sum.
Then write the product.

2 groups of 5

1 $5 + 5 =$ ______ $2 \times 5 =$ ______

4 groups of 3

2 $3 + 3 + 3 + 3 =$ ______ $4 \times 3 =$ ______

5 groups of 2

3 $2 + 2 + 2 + 2 + 2 =$ ______ $5 \times 2 =$ ______

Talk About It ■ Reasoning

What addition sentence is the same as $3 \times 7 = 21$?

Write the sum.
Then write the product.

1. $10 + 10 =$ 20 $\quad 2 \times 10 =$ 20

2. $5 + 5 + 5 =$ _____ $\quad 3 \times 5 =$ _____

3. $1 + 1 + 1 + 1 =$ _____ $\quad 4 \times 1 =$ _____

4. $4 + 4 + 4 + 4 =$ _____ $\quad 4 \times 4 =$ _____

Mixed Review

Add or subtract.

5. Mr. Farley's class sold 256 orchestra tickets.
Ms. Li's class sold 349 orchestra tickets.
How many tickets did the two classes sell in all?

_____ tickets

HOME ACTIVITY • **Have your child set out pennies in 5 groups of 5, count by fives to find the total amount, and say the multiplication sentence.**

Name ______________________________

UNDERSTAND PLAN SOLVE CHECK

Jason puts his counters in equal rows.
He makes 2 rows. He puts 5 counters in each row. How many counters does Jason have?

UNDERSTAND

What do you want to find out?

PLAN

You can make a model to solve the problem.

SOLVE

Use ●. Make a model.

Since there are equal rows, you can multiply.

$2 \times 5 = \underline{10}$

Jason has __10__ counters.

CHECK

Does your answer make sense? Explain.

Use ●. Make a model. Write the product.
Draw a picture to show your work.

1. 3 rows
   4 in each row

   $3 \times 4 = \_\_\_\_$

Use ●. Make a model.
Write the product.

1

6 rows

5 in each row

$6 \times 5 =$ 30

2

______ rows

______ in each row

$4 \times 4 =$ ______

3

______ rows

______ in each row

$5 \times 2 =$ ______

4

______ rows

______ in each row

$5 \times 1 =$ ______

5

______ rows

______ in each row

$6 \times 2 =$ ______

6

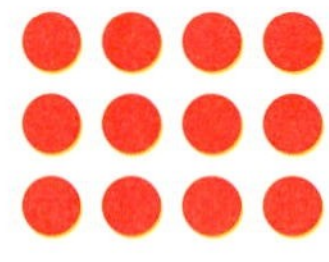

______ rows

______ in each row

$3 \times 4 =$ ______

Problem Solving • Reasoning

7 Change the rows to make equal groups.

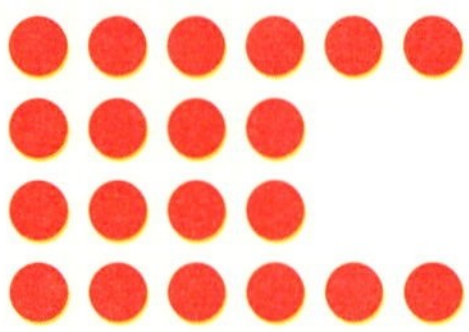

Draw the new picture.

Write the numbers.

______ rows

______ in each row

___ × ___ = ___

HOME ACTIVITY • With your child, use pennies to make arrays. For example, show 4 rows with 3 pennies in each row. Have your child write the multiplication problem and then find the product. Repeat with other arrays.

Name ______________________

Multiply in Any Order

These **multiplication sentences** use the Order Property. The same numbers are multiplied in a different order.

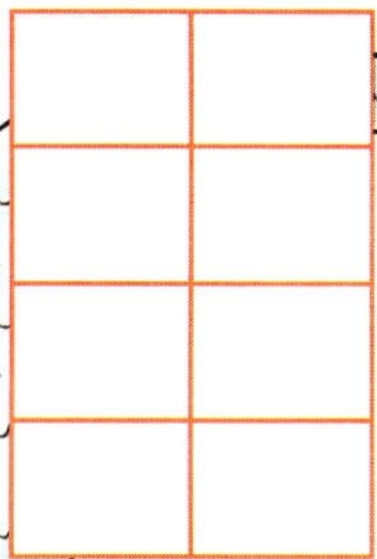

4 rows

2 in each row

4 × 2 = 8

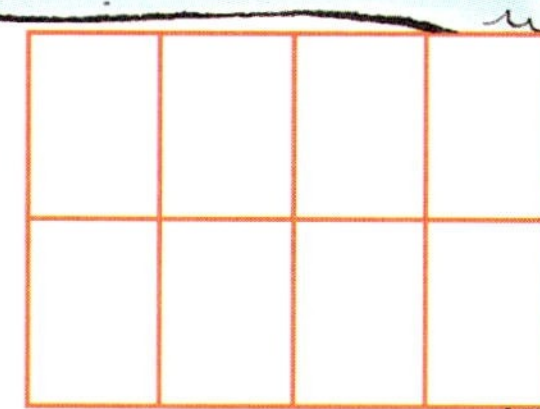

2 rows

4 in each row

2 × 4 = 8

Write how many.
Write the product.

1

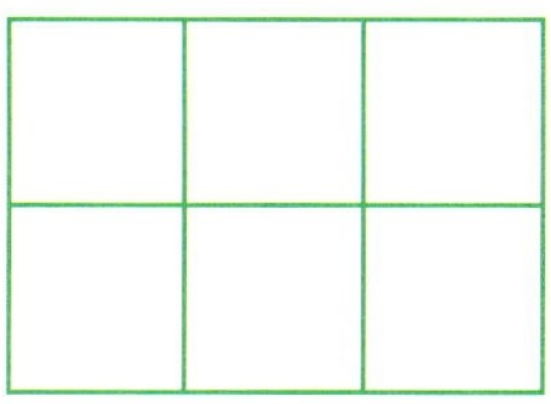

____ rows

____ in each row

____ × ____ = ____

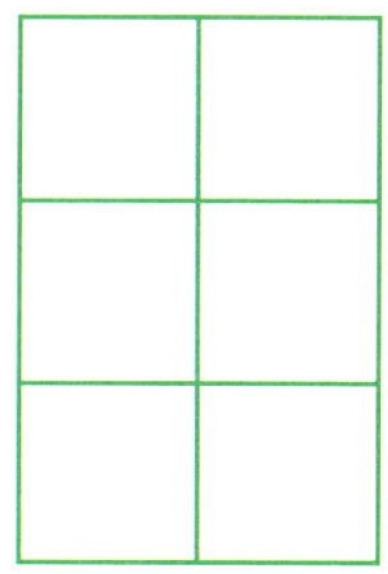

____ rows

____ in each row

____ × ____ = ____

2

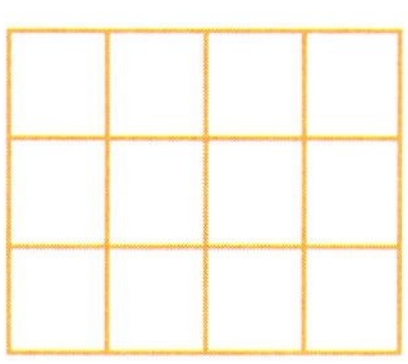

____ rows

____ in each row

____ × ____ = ____

____ rows

____ in each row

____ × ____ = ____

Talk About It ■ **Reasoning**

What is a way to see that 5 × 3 and 3 × 5 have the same product?

Write the product.
Write the multiplication fact in a different order.

1. $4 \times 3 = \underline{12}$
   $\underline{3} \times \underline{4} = \underline{12}$

2. $10 \times 2 = \_\_\_\_$
   $\_\_\_\_ \times \_\_\_\_ = \_\_\_\_$

3. $9 \times 3 = \_\_\_\_$
   $\_\_\_\_ \times \_\_\_\_ = \_\_\_\_$

4. $6 \times 4 = \_\_\_\_$
   $\_\_\_\_ \times \_\_\_\_ = \_\_\_\_$

5. $4 \times 10 = \_\_\_\_$
   $\_\_\_\_ \times \_\_\_\_ = \_\_\_\_$

6. $8 \times 4 = \_\_\_\_$
   $\_\_\_\_ \times \_\_\_\_ = \_\_\_\_$

7. $7 \times 2 = \_\_\_\_$
   $\_\_\_\_ \times \_\_\_\_ = \_\_\_\_$

8. $6 \times 5 = \_\_\_\_$
   $\_\_\_\_ \times \_\_\_\_ = \_\_\_\_$

Algebra

Solve. Write the product.

9. If ● × ■ = 15, then ■ × ● = ____

10. If ● × ■ = 24, then ■ × ● = ____

11. If ● × ■ = 50, then ■ × ● = ____

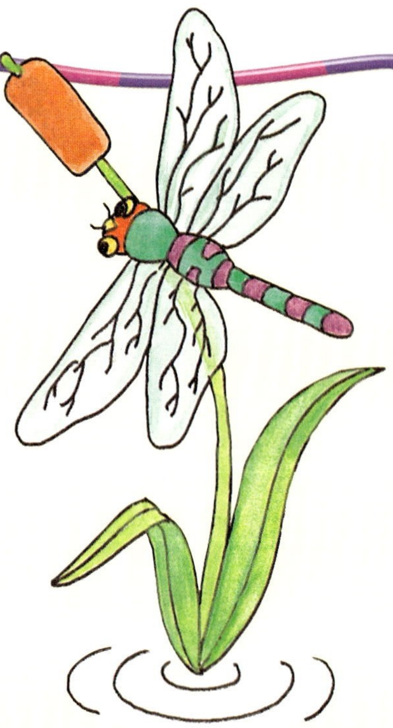

HOME ACTIVITY • Ask your child to explain how the related multiplication sentences on this page are the same (the product is the same, the same numbers are multiplied) and how they are different (the numbers are multiplied in a different order).

Name ____________________

Multiply Across and Down

You can write multiplication facts two ways.

$2 \times 3 = \underline{6}$

groups — frogs in each group — frogs in all

$$\begin{array}{r} 3 \\ \times 2 \\ \hline 6 \end{array}$$

3 frogs in each group

×2 groups

6 frogs in all

Write the product.

1. $4 \times 2 =$ ____ $\quad \begin{array}{r} 2 \\ \times 4 \\ \hline \end{array}$
2. $3 \times 4 =$ ____ $\quad \begin{array}{r} 4 \\ \times 3 \\ \hline \end{array}$
3. $2 \times 5 =$ ____ $\quad \begin{array}{r} 5 \\ \times 2 \\ \hline \end{array}$
4. $6 \times 3 =$ ____ $\quad \begin{array}{r} 3 \\ \times 6 \\ \hline \end{array}$
5. $7 \times 2 =$ ____ $\quad \begin{array}{r} 2 \\ \times 7 \\ \hline \end{array}$
6. $6 \times 5 =$ ____ $\quad \begin{array}{r} 5 \\ \times 6 \\ \hline \end{array}$
7. $5 \times 1 =$ ____ $\quad \begin{array}{r} 1 \\ \times 5 \\ \hline \end{array}$
8. $7 \times 7 =$ ____ $\quad \begin{array}{r} 7 \\ \times 7 \\ \hline \end{array}$
9. $8 \times 4 =$ ____ $\quad \begin{array}{r} 4 \\ \times 8 \\ \hline \end{array}$

Talk About It ▪ Reasoning

Why is the product the same when you multiply 2×3 and 3×2?

Write the product.

1. $3 \times 10 =$ 30

$$\begin{array}{r} 10 \\ \times 3 \\ \hline 30 \end{array}$$

2. $6 \times 2 =$ ____

$$\begin{array}{r} 2 \\ \times 6 \\ \hline \end{array}$$

3. $4 \times 5 =$ ____

$$\begin{array}{r} 5 \\ \times 4 \\ \hline \end{array}$$

4. $9 \times 3 =$ ____

$$\begin{array}{r} 3 \\ \times 9 \\ \hline \end{array}$$

5. $7 \times 10 =$ ____

$$\begin{array}{r} 10 \\ \times 7 \\ \hline \end{array}$$

6. $6 \times 5 =$ ____

$$\begin{array}{r} 5 \\ \times 6 \\ \hline \end{array}$$

7. $8 \times 2 =$ ____

$$\begin{array}{r} 2 \\ \times 8 \\ \hline \end{array}$$

8. $7 \times 1 =$ ____

$$\begin{array}{r} 1 \\ \times 7 \\ \hline \end{array}$$

9. $4 \times 4 =$ ____

$$\begin{array}{r} 4 \\ \times 4 \\ \hline \end{array}$$

Problem Solving ■ Application

Write a multiplication sentence to show your answer.

10. Janie has 5 nickels.
If she traded the nickels for pennies, how many pennies would she have?

____ × ____ = ____ pennies

HOME ACTIVITY • Write any multiplication sentence in horizontal format, and ask your child to write the same multiplication fact in vertical format. Repeat several times with different multiplication facts.

Name ______________________

CHECK ■ Concepts and Skills

Make equal groups of ■.
Skip-count. Write how many in all.

1. Make 6 equal groups.
   Put 10 ■ in each group.

_____, _____, _____, _____, _____, _____ _____ in all

Write the sum.
Then write the product.

2. $5 + 5 =$ _____ $2 \times 5 =$ _____

Write the product.
Write the multiplication fact in a different order.

3. $6 \times 4 =$ _____

   _____ $\times$ _____ $=$ _____

4. $7 \times 5 =$ _____

   _____ $\times$ _____ $=$ _____

Write the product.

5. $9 \times 2 =$ _____

$$\begin{array}{r} 2 \\ \times 9 \\ \hline \end{array}$$

6. $7 \times 3 =$ _____

$$\begin{array}{r} 3 \\ \times 7 \\ \hline \end{array}$$

7. $8 \times 10 =$ _____

$$\begin{array}{r} 10 \\ \times 8 \\ \hline \end{array}$$

CHECK ■ Problem Solving

Use ●. Make a model. Write the product.

8. 

   _____ rows

   _____ in each row

   $6 \times 2 =$ _____

Name ______________________________

Choose the best answer for questions 1–4.

1 Which shows another way to find 2 + 2 + 2?

3 × 2	3 × 3	2 + 2	2 + 3
○	○	○	○

2 Which shows the product?

4 rows
4 in each row

12	15	16	20
○	○	○	○

3 Which has the same product as 7 × 3?

2 × 7	3 × 2	7 × 2	3 × 7
○	○	○	○

4

$$\begin{array}{r} 27 \\ +\ 19 \\ \hline \end{array}$$

12	36	46	56
○	○	○	○

Show What You Know

5 Draw a garden. Make 5 rows.
Put the same number in each row.
Write a multiplication sentence that tells how many there are in all.

_____ × _____ = _____

Multiplication Facts 2, 5, and 10

Look for equal groups. Write multiplication facts about them.

SCHOOL HOME CONNECTION

Dear Family,

Today we started Chapter 29. We will recall the multiplication facts with 2, 5, and 10. Here is the math vocabulary and an activity for us to do together at home.

Love,

____

My Math Word

multiply

Vocabulary

multiply To find out how many in all when you know the number of groups and the number in each group.

These objects are in equal groups.

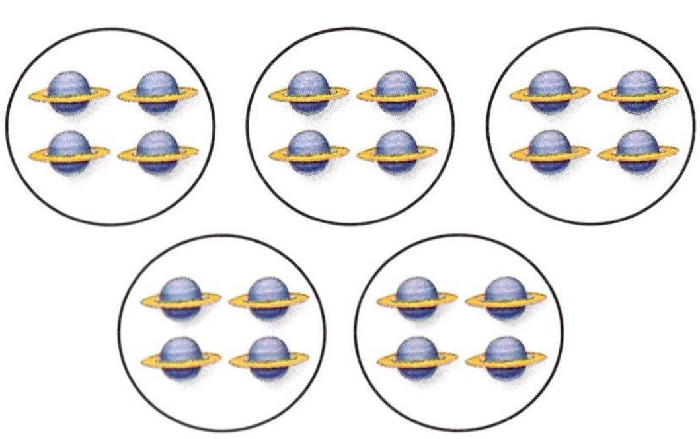

How many are in 5 groups of 4?

4 in each group
$\times 5$ groups
20

Visit *The Learning Site* for additional ideas and activities. www.harcourtschool.com

ACTIVITY

When in the supermarket, pick up an item that has 10 items in one package. For example, if 10 bars come in a box, ask your child to use multiplication to tell how many bars would be in three boxes. Do the same with other items.

Books to Share

To read about multiplication with your child, look for these books in your local library.

Anno's Mysterious Multiplying Jar, by Masaichiro and Mitsumasa Anno, Putnam & Grosset Group, 1983.

Shoes, Shoes, Shoes, by Anne Morris, William Morrow & Company, 1998.

Can You Count Ten Toes?, by Lezlie Evans, Houghton Mifflin, 1998.

Name ______________________________

Multiply with 2

There are 7 groups of 2 wheels.
How many wheels are there in all?
Skip-count.

You can skip-count by twos to find the product.

2, 4, 6, 8, 10, 12, 14

$7 \times 2 =$ 14 wheels

You can multiply to find the product.

How many wheels are there in all?
Write the product.

1

$1 \times 2 =$ ______

$2 \times 2 =$ ______

$3 \times 2 =$ ______

2

$4 \times 2 =$ ______

$5 \times 2 =$ ______

$6 \times 2 =$ ______

Talk About It ■ **Reasoning**

Why could you use doubles to solve these problems?

Write the product.

1

$7 \times 2 =$ 14

$8 \times 2 =$ ______

$9 \times 2 =$ ______

2 $\begin{array}{r} 2 \\ \times 1 \\ \hline 2 \end{array}$ $\begin{array}{r} 1 \\ \times 2 \\ \hline \end{array}$ $\begin{array}{r} 2 \\ \times 2 \\ \hline \end{array}$ $\begin{array}{r} 2 \\ \times 3 \\ \hline \end{array}$ $\begin{array}{r} 3 \\ \times 2 \\ \hline \end{array}$ $\begin{array}{r} 2 \\ \times 4 \\ \hline \end{array}$ $\begin{array}{r} 4 \\ \times 2 \\ \hline \end{array}$

3 $\begin{array}{r} 2 \\ \times 5 \\ \hline \end{array}$ $\begin{array}{r} 5 \\ \times 2 \\ \hline \end{array}$ $\begin{array}{r} 2 \\ \times 6 \\ \hline \end{array}$ $\begin{array}{r} 6 \\ \times 2 \\ \hline \end{array}$ $\begin{array}{r} 2 \\ \times 7 \\ \hline \end{array}$ $\begin{array}{r} 7 \\ \times 2 \\ \hline \end{array}$

4 $\begin{array}{r} 2 \\ \times 8 \\ \hline \end{array}$ $\begin{array}{r} 8 \\ \times 2 \\ \hline \end{array}$ $\begin{array}{r} 2 \\ \times 9 \\ \hline \end{array}$ $\begin{array}{r} 9 \\ \times 2 \\ \hline \end{array}$ $\begin{array}{r} 2 \\ \times 10 \\ \hline \end{array}$ $\begin{array}{r} 10 \\ \times 2 \\ \hline \end{array}$

Problem Solving ■ Visual Thinking

5 Write the multiplication sentence that this number line shows.

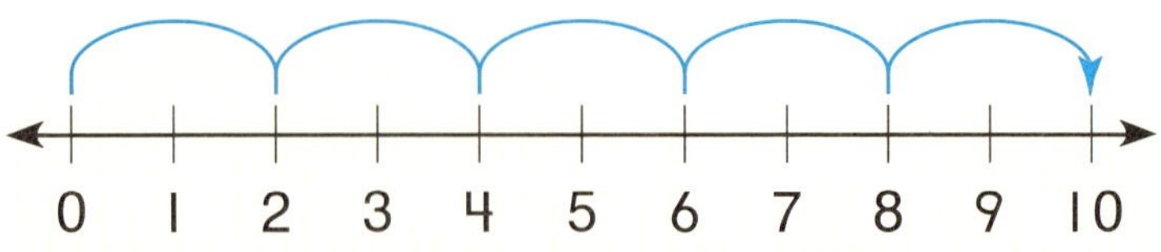

______ × ______ = ______

HOME ACTIVITY • Give your child a multiplication problem with 2, for example, 6 × 2. Ask your child to name the product. Repeat with different problems with 2 until your child has memorized the facts.

Name ______________________________

Multiply with 5

There are 8 groups of 5 fingers.
How many fingers are there in all?
Skip-count.

You can skip-count by fives to find the product.

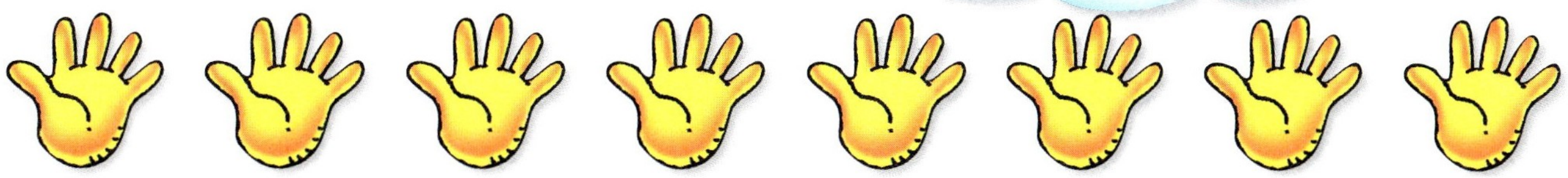

5, 10, 15, 20, 25, 30, 35, 40

$8 \times 5 =$ 40 fingers

You can multiply to find the product.

How many fingers are there in all?
Write the product.

1

$1 \times 5 =$ ______

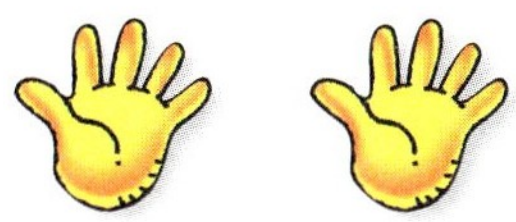

$2 \times 5 =$ ______

$3 \times 5 =$ ______

2

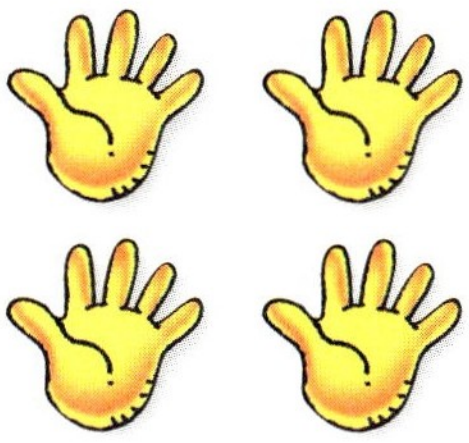

$4 \times 5 =$ ______

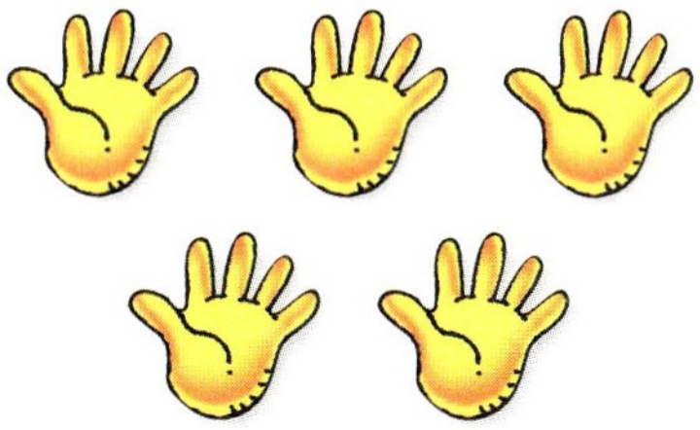

$5 \times 5 =$ ______

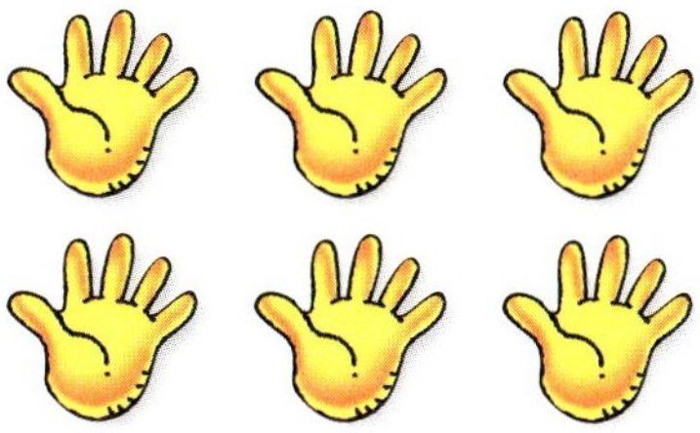

$6 \times 5 =$ ______

Talk About It ■ Reasoning
What patterns do you see when you multiply with 5?

How many fingers are there in all?
Write the product.

1

$7 \times 5 =$ 35	$8 \times 5 =$ ____	$9 \times 5 =$ ____

Write the product.

2

$\begin{array}{r} 5 \\ \times 1 \\ \hline 5 \end{array}$	$\begin{array}{r} 1 \\ \times 5 \\ \hline \end{array}$	$\begin{array}{r} 5 \\ \times 2 \\ \hline \end{array}$	$\begin{array}{r} 2 \\ \times 5 \\ \hline \end{array}$	$\begin{array}{r} 5 \\ \times 3 \\ \hline \end{array}$	$\begin{array}{r} 3 \\ \times 5 \\ \hline \end{array}$

3

$\begin{array}{r} 5 \\ \times 4 \\ \hline \end{array}$	$\begin{array}{r} 4 \\ \times 5 \\ \hline \end{array}$	$\begin{array}{r} 5 \\ \times 6 \\ \hline \end{array}$	$\begin{array}{r} 6 \\ \times 5 \\ \hline \end{array}$	$\begin{array}{r} 7 \\ \times 5 \\ \hline \end{array}$	$\begin{array}{r} 5 \\ \times 7 \\ \hline \end{array}$

Algebra

Look for a pattern. Write the missing numbers.

4

$\begin{array}{r} 5 \\ \times 1 \\ \hline \square \end{array}$	$\begin{array}{r} 5 \\ \times \square \\ \hline 10 \end{array}$	$\begin{array}{r} 5 \\ \times 3 \\ \hline \square \end{array}$	$\begin{array}{r} 5 \\ \times \square \\ \hline 20 \end{array}$	$\begin{array}{r} \square \\ \times 5 \\ \hline 25 \end{array}$	$\begin{array}{r} 5 \\ \times \square \\ \hline 30 \end{array}$

HOME ACTIVITY • Give your child a multiplication problem with 5, for example, 8 × 5. Ask your child to name the product. Repeat with different problems with 5 until your child has memorized the facts.

Name ______________________________

Multiply with 10

There are 3 groups of 10 counters.
How many counters are there in all?
Skip-count.

You can skip-count by tens to find the product.

$3 \times 10 =$ 30 counters

You can multiply to find the product.

How many counters are there in all?
Write the product.

1. $1 \times 10 =$ ______

2. $2 \times 10 =$ ______

3. $3 \times 10 =$ ______

4. $4 \times 10 =$ ______

5. $5 \times 10 =$ ______

6. $6 \times 10 =$ ______

Talk About It ▪ Reasoning

What patterns do you see when you multiply with 10?

How many counters are there in all?
Write the product.

1 

$7 \times 10 =$ 70

2 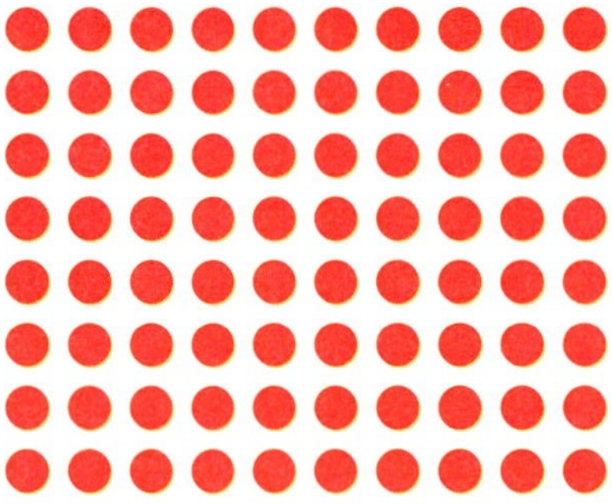

$8 \times 10 =$ ____

3 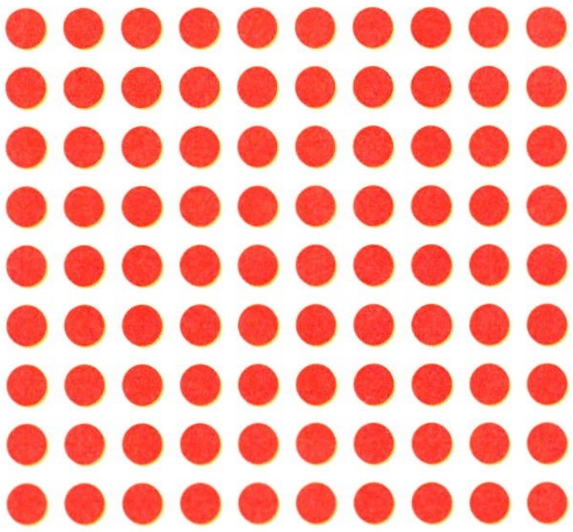

$9 \times 10 =$ ____

4 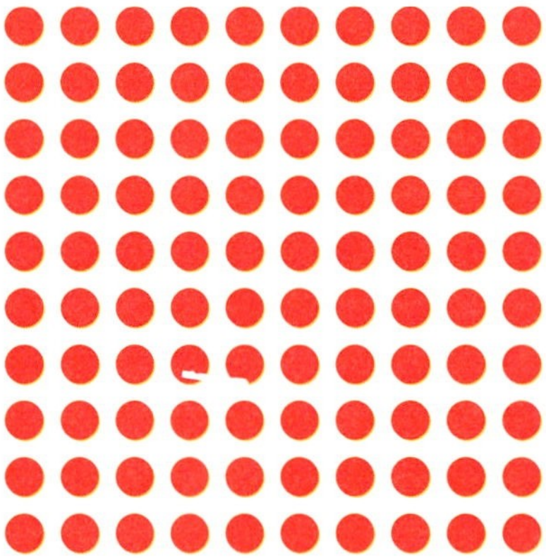

$10 \times 10 =$ ____

Write the product.

5 $\begin{array}{r} 10 \\ \times 8 \\ \hline \end{array}$ $\begin{array}{r} 10 \\ \times 2 \\ \hline \end{array}$ $\begin{array}{r} 10 \\ \times 1 \\ \hline \end{array}$ $\begin{array}{r} 10 \\ \times 5 \\ \hline \end{array}$ $\begin{array}{r} 4 \\ \times 10 \\ \hline \end{array}$ $\begin{array}{r} 6 \\ \times 10 \\ \hline \end{array}$

6 $\begin{array}{r} 10 \\ \times 9 \\ \hline \end{array}$ $\begin{array}{r} 5 \\ \times 10 \\ \hline \end{array}$ $\begin{array}{r} 10 \\ \times 7 \\ \hline \end{array}$ $\begin{array}{r} 3 \\ \times 10 \\ \hline \end{array}$ $\begin{array}{r} 1 \\ \times 10 \\ \hline \end{array}$ $\begin{array}{r} 10 \\ \times 10 \\ \hline \end{array}$

HOME ACTIVITY • Give your child a multiplication problem with 10, for example, 5×10. Ask your child to name the product. Repeat with different problems with 10 until your child has memorized the facts.

Name ______________________________

UNDERSTAND **PLAN** **SOLVE** **CHECK**

?	
2	4
3	6
4	8

UNDERSTAND

What do you want to find out?

PLAN

You can use logical reasoning to find the pattern and write a rule.

SOLVE

Multiply 2	
2	4
3	6
4	8

CHECK

Does your answer make sense? Explain.

Write the rule.

1

0	0
1	5
2	10

2

5	50
6	60
7	70

Write the rule.

1

1	2
2	4
3	6
4	8
5	10

2

5	50
6	60
7	70
8	80
9	90

3

6	30
7	35
8	40
9	45
10	50

4 Complete the table.

×	1	2	3	4	5	6	7	8	9	10
2	2									
5										
10										

Problem Solving ▪ Reasoning

5 Jorge drinks 5 glasses of milk a day. How much milk does he drink in a week?

_______ glasses

HOME ACTIVITY • Each day, work with your child for a short time on multiplication facts. For example, find the value for groups of nickels or dimes by using multiplication. 5 nickels is $5 \times 5 = 25$.

Name ______________________________

CHECK ■ Concepts and Skills

How many fingers are there in all?
Write the product.

1

$3 \times 5 =$ _____

$5 \times 5 =$ _____

$7 \times 5 =$ _____

Write the product.

2

$\begin{array}{r} 5 \\ \times 5 \\ \hline \end{array}$ $\begin{array}{r} 5 \\ \times 2 \\ \hline \end{array}$ $\begin{array}{r} 10 \\ \times 5 \\ \hline \end{array}$ $\begin{array}{r} 3 \\ \times 5 \\ \hline \end{array}$ $\begin{array}{r} 5 \\ \times 9 \\ \hline \end{array}$ $\begin{array}{r} 4 \\ \times 5 \\ \hline \end{array}$

3

$\begin{array}{r} 1 \\ \times 10 \\ \hline \end{array}$ $\begin{array}{r} 10 \\ \times 9 \\ \hline \end{array}$ $\begin{array}{r} 4 \\ \times 10 \\ \hline \end{array}$ $\begin{array}{r} 10 \\ \times 4 \\ \hline \end{array}$ $\begin{array}{r} 3 \\ \times 10 \\ \hline \end{array}$ $\begin{array}{r} 10 \\ \times 10 \\ \hline \end{array}$

Multiply.

4

$\begin{array}{r} 9 \\ \times 5 \\ \hline \end{array}$ $\begin{array}{r} 10 \\ \times 8 \\ \hline \end{array}$ $\begin{array}{r} 7 \\ \times 5 \\ \hline \end{array}$ $\begin{array}{r} 2 \\ \times 5 \\ \hline \end{array}$ $\begin{array}{r} 5 \\ \times 6 \\ \hline \end{array}$ $\begin{array}{r} 2 \\ \times 10 \\ \hline \end{array}$

CHECK ■ Problem Solving

Write the rule.

5

1	10
2	20
3	30

6

6	12
7	14
8	16

Name ______________________

Choose the best answer for questions 1–7.

1 2×9

- 14
- 16
- 18
- 19

2 5×4

- 16
- 20
- 22
- 25

3 10×1

- 10
- 11
- 20
- 100

4 6×2

- 0
- 12
- 35
- 36

5 5×8

- 13
- 35
- 40
- 45

6 10×2

- 2
- 12
- 20
- 30

7 A collie weighs 100 pounds. A beagle weighs 35 pounds. A bloodhound weighs 180 pounds. How much do the collie and the beagle weigh together?

- 45 pounds
- 135 pounds
- 280 pounds
- 315 pounds

Show What You Know

8 Finish the table.
Write a rule.
Write numbers that follow the rule.

Multiply ____	
2	
5	
10	

CHAPTER 30 Division Concepts

Share the party items equally among the children. How many will each child get?

SCHOOL HOME CONNECTION

Dear Family,

Today we started Chapter 30. We will begin to learn about division. Here is the math vocabulary and an activity for us to do together at home.

Love,

____

My Math Words

divide

quotient

Vocabulary

divide To separate a group of objects into equal smaller groups.

$$6 \div 3 = 2$$

↑ division symbol

Read as *six divided by three equals two.*

quotient The answer in a division problem.

$$20 \div 5 = 4$$

↑ quotient

Visit ***The Learning Site*** **for additional ideas and activities.**
www.harcourtschool.com

ACTIVITY

Give your child dried beans to divide into equal groups. Cut egg cartons into 3-cup, 4-cup, and 5-cup sections. Have your child count out 15 beans into the 3-cup section, forming 3 equal groups. Ask how many beans are in each cup. Repeat, using different numbers of beans and cups.

Books to Share

To read about division with your child, look for these books in your local library.

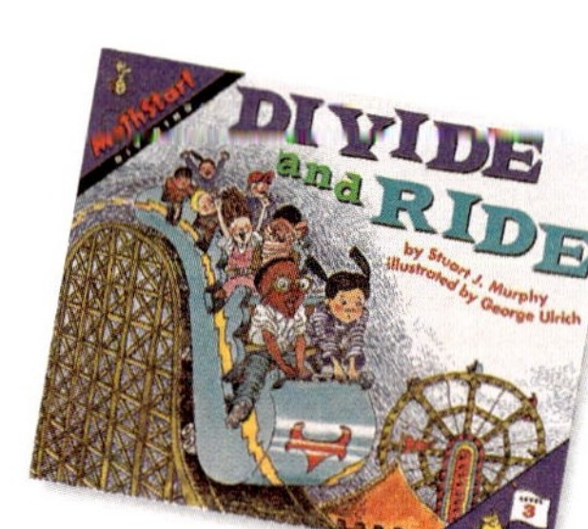

Divide and Ride,
by Stuart J. Murphy,
HarperCollins, 1997.

Madeline,
by Ludwig Bemelmans,
Penguin, 2000.

Name ______________________________

Equal Shares

Circle equal groups.
How many are in each group?
How many are left over?

1 **Divide** 12 flowers into 3 equal groups.

4 in each group   0 left over

2 Divide 13 oranges into 2 equal groups.

6 in each group   1 left over

3 Divide 15 cookies into 3 equal groups.

______ in each group   ______ left over

Talk About It ■ Reasoning

There are 15 pennies. Patrice divides them into equal groups and has 0 left over. Al divides them into equal groups and has 1 left over. What may be the reason?

Circle equal groups. How many are in each group?
How many are left over?

1 Divide 10 party hats into 3 equal groups.

3 in each group 1 left over

2 Divide 14 balloons into 4 equal groups.

_____ in each group _____ left over

3 Divide 18 whistles into 4 equal groups.

_____ in each group _____ left over

Problem Solving ▪ Reasoning

4 There are 14 toys and 4 children.
Each child gets the same number of toys.
How many toys does each child get? _____ toys

How many more toys would be needed
for each child to get another toy? _____ toys

HOME ACTIVITY • Ask your child to explain how he or she found the answer for each problem in this lesson.

Name ______________________________

Make Equal Groups

Circle equal groups.
How many groups are there?
How many are left over?

1 Divide 10 coins into groups of 5.

__2__ groups   __0__ left over

2 Divide 14 apples into groups of 6.

_______ groups   _______ left over

3 Divide 13 balloons into groups of 3.

_______ groups   _______ left over

4 Divide 10 peanuts into groups of 2.

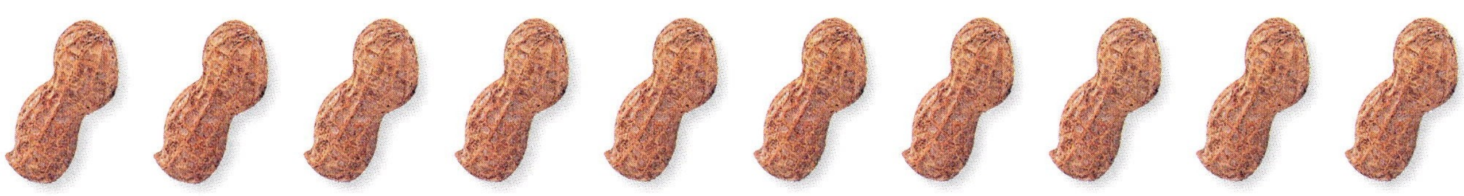

_______ groups   _______ left over

Talk About It ▪ Reasoning

You have 12 plums. How many ways can you make equal groups with no plums left over?

Circle equal groups.
How many groups are there?
How many are left over?

1 Divide 16 cups into groups of 4.

__4__ groups __0__ left over

2 Divide 11 napkins into groups of 3.

______ groups ______ left over

3 Divide 15 forks into groups of 4.

______ groups ______ left over

Problem Solving ■ Visual Thinking

4 There are 15 pencils. Each child gets 2 pencils.

How many children are there? ______ children

How many pencils are left over? ______ left over

HOME ACTIVITY • Have your child use small items, such as paper clips, to make equal groups.

Name ______________________

Subtraction and Division

Hands On

There are 8 counters.
How many groups of 2 counters can you make?

8	÷	2	=	?
number of counters		number in each group		number of groups

Start with 8.
Take away groups of 2 until you get 0.

$\begin{array}{r} 8 \\ -\ 2 \\ \hline 6 \end{array}$	$\begin{array}{r} 6 \\ -\ 2 \\ \hline 4 \end{array}$	$\begin{array}{r} 4 \\ -\ 2 \\ \hline 2 \end{array}$	$\begin{array}{r} 2 \\ -\ 2 \\ \hline 0 \end{array}$

You can subtract 2 from 8 four times, since there are 4 groups of 2 in 8.

$8 \div 2 =$ <u>4</u>

Show the total with ●. Subtract the number in each group. Write the differences and the quotient.

1 You have 20 ●. Make groups of 5.

$\begin{array}{r} 20 \\ -\ 5 \\ \hline \end{array}$ $\begin{array}{r} 15 \\ -\ 5 \\ \hline \end{array}$ $\begin{array}{r} 10 \\ -\ 5 \\ \hline \end{array}$ $\begin{array}{r} 5 \\ -\ 5 \\ \hline \end{array}$

$20 \div 5 =$ ______

2 You have 9 ●. Make groups of 3.

$\begin{array}{r} 9 \\ -\ 3 \\ \hline \end{array}$ $\begin{array}{r} 6 \\ -\ 3 \\ \hline \end{array}$ $\begin{array}{r} 3 \\ -\ 3 \\ \hline \end{array}$

$9 \div 3 =$ ______

Talk About It ■ Reasoning
How is subtracting over and over like division?

Use subtraction to find the quotient.

1 You have 12 ●. Make groups of 2.

12	10	8	6	4	2
− **2**	− **2**	− **2**	− **2**	− **2**	− **2**
10	8	6	4	2	0

$12 \div 2 =$ 6

2 You have 15 ●. Make groups of 5.

15	10	5
− **5**	− **5**	− **5**

$15 \div 5 =$ ______

3 You have 20 ●. Make groups of 10.

20	10
− **10**	− **10**

$20 \div 10 =$ ______

4 You have 18 ●. Make groups of 3.

18	15	12	9	6	3
− **3**	− **3**	− **3**	− **3**	− **3**	− **3**

$18 \div 3 =$ ______

Mixed Review

Add or subtract.

5

tens	ones
□	□
9	4
−3	7

6

tens	ones
□	
3	2
+3	8

7

tens	ones
□	
1	6
+3	7

8

tens	ones
□	□
4	1
−1	6

HOME ACTIVITY • Give your child 12 pennies, and ask how many groups of 6 pennies he or she can make. Help your child make 2 groups of 6 and write $12 - 6 = 6$, $6 - 6 = 0$, so $12 \div 6 = 2$.

Name ____________________

UNDERSTAND ▸ PLAN ▸ SOLVE ▸ CHECK

Circle the number sentence that makes sense for the problem. Then solve.

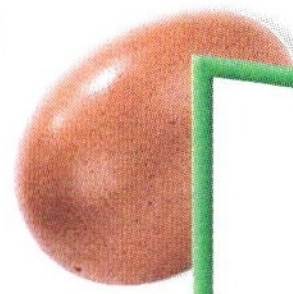

1 Jana has 6 hens. On Monday, each hen laid 4 eggs. How many eggs were laid on Monday?

24 eggs

$6 + 4 =$ ______

$6 \times 4 =$ 24

2 Mr. Jones has 853 cows. Mr. Peters has 539 cows. How many more cows does Mr. Jones have than Mr. Peters?

______ more cows

$853 - 539 =$ ______

$853 + 539 =$ ______

3 Craig planted 15 seeds in 5 minutes. How many seeds can he plant in 1 minute?

______ seeds

$15 - 5 =$ ______

$15 \div 5 =$ ______

4 Arial has $4.67. She buys seeds for $2.80. How much money does she have left?

______

$\$4.67 \times \$2.80 =$ ______

$\$4.67 - \$2.80 =$ ______

5 There are 24 hours in a day. Each class is 4 hours long. How many classes could you take in a day?

______ classes

$24 \times 4 =$ ______

$24 \div 4 =$ ______

Circle the number sentence that makes sense for the problem. Then solve.

1 Ali has put stamps in a book. The book has 10 pages. Each page holds 2 stamps. How many stamps are in the book?

20 stamps

$10 \times 2 =$ 20 (circled)

$10 \div 2 =$ ____

2 Mr. Lucky has 46 big boxes and 21 small boxes on the shelf. How many more big boxes are there than little boxes?

____ more big boxes

$46 + 21 =$ ____

$46 - 21 =$ ____

3 There are 16 cookies. Four friends share the cookies equally. How many cookies does each friend get?

____ cookies

$16 - 4 =$ ____

$16 \div 4 =$ ____

4 Maria has 15 pictures. If she gives 3 pictures to each friend, how many friends get pictures?

____ friends

$15 \div 3 =$ ____

$15 \times 4 =$ ____

Math Journal

Write About It

Make up your own math story problem. You can add, subtract, multiply, or divide. Ask a classmate to solve it.

HOME ACTIVITY • With your child, look at the exercises in this lesson. Ask your child to explain how he or she decided whether to add, subtract, multiply, or divide.

Name ______________________________

UNDERSTAND PLAN SOLVE CHECK

Mrs. Bear has 12 plums.
She gives 2 to each of her cubs.
How many cubs does she have?

Strategies
Draw a Picture
Make a Model
Make a List

UNDERSTAND

You need to find out how many cubs there are in Mrs. Bear's family.

PLAN

Choose a way to solve the problem.
You could draw a picture.

SOLVE

There are __6__ cubs in Mrs. Bear's family.

CHECK

Does your answer make sense? Explain.

Choose a strategy to solve the problem.

1. Juan has 20¢. He finds 15¢ more. If one peach costs 5¢, how many peaches can Juan buy?

   _______ peaches

2. There are 32 plants. If Craig plants them in 4 equal rows, how many plants will be in each row?

   _______ plants

Choose a strategy to solve the problem.

Strategies
Draw a Picture
Make a Model
Make a List

1. Liz has $9.00.
Tickets cost $3.00 each.
How many tickets can Liz buy?

3 tickets

2. Kathy has 30 coins in her collection.
She stacks her coins in 3 equal piles.
How many coins are in each pile?

_______ coins

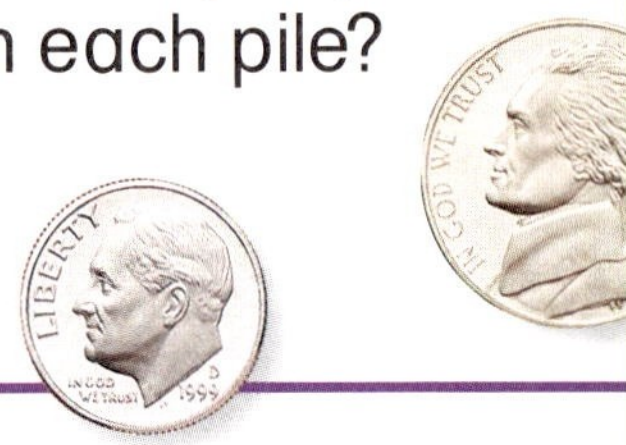

3. Leroy has 5 red apples and 5 green apples. He gives 2 apples to each of his friends.
How many friends get apples?

_______ friends

4. Mary has 10 red flowers and 2 pink flowers. She puts her flowers in 4 vases. How many flowers are in each vase?

_______ flowers

Write About It

Make up your own math story problem. Ask a classmate to solve it. He or she can choose any strategy to solve the problem.

HOME ACTIVITY • **Make up addition, subtraction, multiplication, and division problems for your child to solve.**

Name ______________________

CHECK ▪ Concepts and Skills

1. Divide 14 counters into 3 equal groups. Circle the groups.

How many counters in each group? ______ counters

How many left over? ______

Circle equal groups. How many groups are there? How many are left over?

2. Divide 10 pennies into groups of 2.

______ groups ______ left over

Use subtraction to find the quotient. Write the differences and the quotient.

3. You have 10 ●. Make groups of 2.

$10 - 2$ → $8 - 2$ → $6 - 2$ → $4 - 2$ → $2 - 2$

$10 \div 2 =$ ______

CHECK ▪ Problem Solving

Choose a strategy to solve the problem.

4. There are 9 raisins and 3 boys. Each boy gets an equal number of raisins. How many raisins does each boy get?

______ raisins

Strategies
Draw a Picture
Make a Model
Make a List

Name ______________________________

Choose the best answer for questions 1–4.

1 Which tells about 17 ● divided into 4 equal groups?

●●●● ●●●● ●●●● ●●●● ●

3 in each group 5 left over	4 in each group 2 left over	4 in each group 0 left over	4 in each group 1 left over
○	○	○	○

2 Which tells about 6 ● divided into 3 equal groups?

●● ●● ●●

3 in each group 2 left over	1 in each group 2 left over	2 in each group 0 left over	2 in each group 1 left over
○	○	○	○

3 Corey has 12 muffins. He gives them equally to 6 friends. Which tells how many muffins each friend can have?

12×6	$12 + 6$	$12 \div 6$	$12 - 6$
○	○		○

4 Patricia has 24 puzzle pieces. She puts 16 of them in the puzzle. How many pieces are left?

4	8	18	40
○	○	○	○

Show What You Know

5 Draw 20 stars. Show two ways to put them in equal groups. Write the numbers.

____ groups ____ in each group

____ groups ____ in each group

Can I Play?

written by Ann Lee Earnshaw

illustrated by Ed Martinez

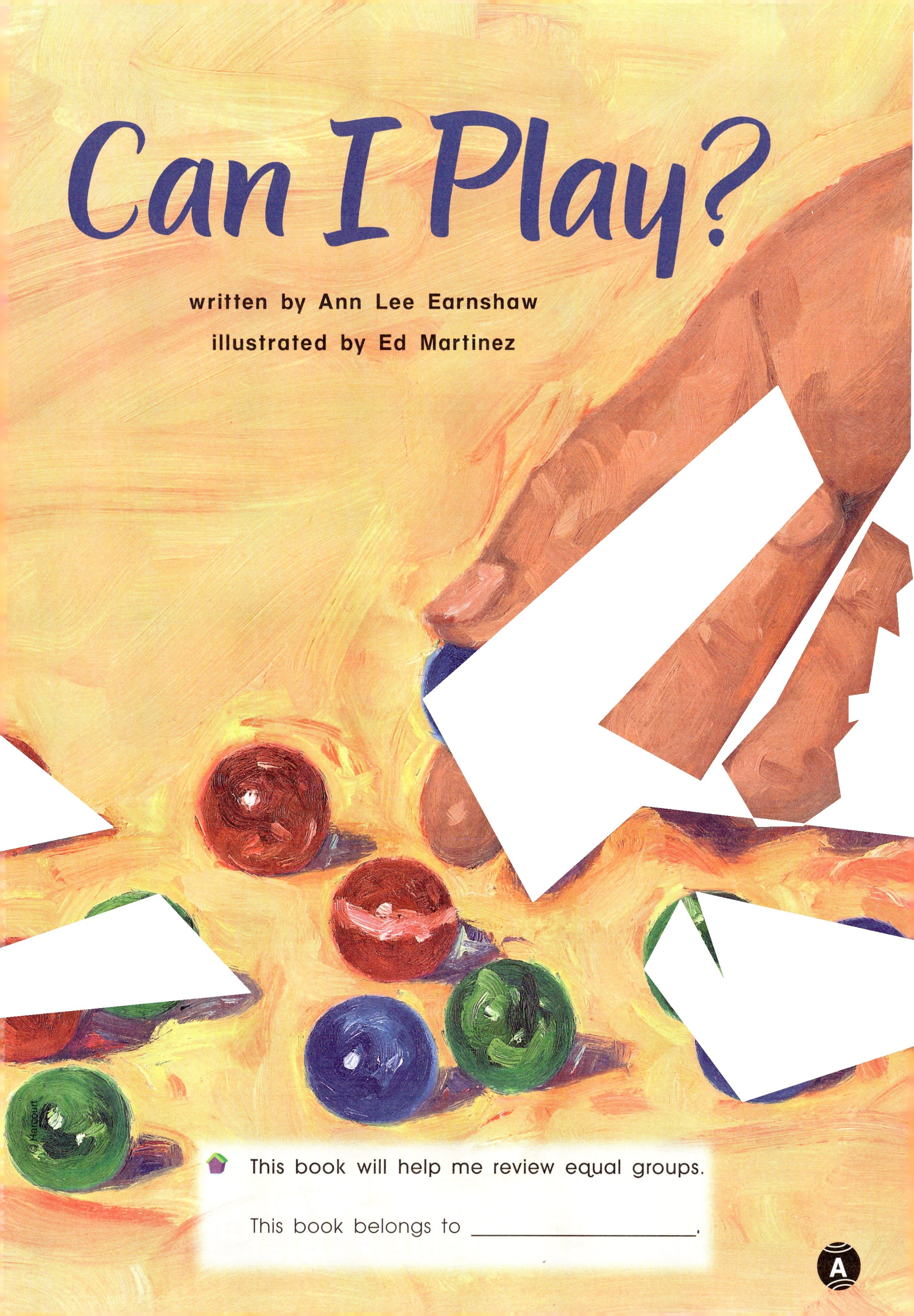

This book will help me review equal groups.

This book belongs to ____________________.

A

Rebecca has 12 marbles.

She wants to share them equally with John.

"Here are ______ marbles for you

and ______ marbles for me," said Rebecca.

"That's fair," said John. "Now can we play?"

B

They were just about to
start the game when Melissa and Jeff
came over. "Can we play?" asked Melissa.
"Yes, you can play," said Rebecca.

"Here are ______ marbles for you, Jeff,

and ______ marbles for you, Melissa,

and ______ marbles for you, John,

and ______ marbles for me," said Rebecca.

They were just about to start the game
when Tom and Susan came over.
"Can we play?" they asked.
"Yes, you can play," said Rebecca.
"Now how many marbles will we get?"
asked Jeff.
"Each of us will get ______
marbles," said Rebecca.

“That’s fair,” said John. “Let’s play!”

Name ______________________

Watch Your Step!

Use your skills to find your way home. Write the missing addition, subtraction, multiplication and division signs as you follow the path.

Talk about It ▪ Explain how you found your way home.

Name ________________________________

Challenge
True/False

$14 + 6 = 21$
This statement is false.
$14 + 6 = 20$
Now this statement is true.

Mark each number sentence as true or false.
If the statement is false, correct it so that it is true.

1	$3 \times 2 = 6$	True	False
2	$14 + 16 = 110$	True	False
3	$10 \div 5 = 2$	True	False
4	$8 + 3 = 10$	True	False
5	$15 < 18$	True	False
6	2 quarters = 5 dimes	True	False
7	$128 + 134 = 261$	True	False
8	$96 - 56 = 40$	True	False
9	$8 \times 4 = 24$	True	False
10	$100 > 200$	True	False

Name ______________________________

Skills and Concepts

Add.

1

$$\begin{array}{r} 4 \\ +3 \\ \hline \end{array} \qquad \begin{array}{r} 4 \text{ hundreds} \\ +3 \text{ hundreds} \\ \hline \end{array} \qquad \begin{array}{r} 400 \\ +300 \\ \hline \end{array}$$

2

hundreds	tens	ones
	□	
3	5	6
+ 2	1	8

3 916 + 16 = ______

Subtract.

4

$$\begin{array}{r} 6 \\ -1 \\ \hline \end{array} \qquad \begin{array}{r} 6 \text{ hundred} \\ -1 \text{ hundred} \\ \hline \end{array} \qquad \begin{array}{r} 600 \\ -100 \\ \hline \end{array}$$

5

hundreds	tens	ones
□	□	□
8	2	2
− 2	0	6

6

hundreds	tens	ones
□	□	□
1	6	8
− 1	4	9

Add or subtract.

7

$$\begin{array}{r} \$5.90 \\ -\$2.89 \\ \hline \end{array}$$

8

$$\begin{array}{r} \$1.45 \\ +\$1.00 \\ \hline \end{array}$$

9

$$\begin{array}{r} 52 \\ +189 \\ \hline \end{array}$$

10

$$\begin{array}{r} 492 \\ -385 \\ \hline \end{array}$$

11 Write the sum. Then write the product.

4 + 4 + 4 = ______ 3 × 4 = ______

12 Write how many rows and how many in each row.
Then write the product.

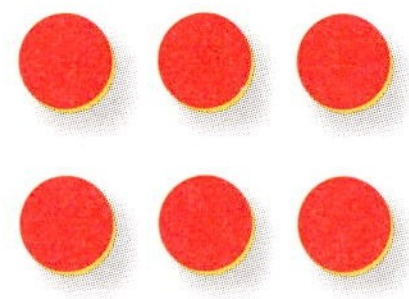

_____ rows _____ in each row

_____ $\times$ _____ = _____

13 $5 \times 3 =$ _____

$$\begin{array}{r} 3 \\ \times 5 \\ \hline \end{array}$$

14

$$\begin{array}{r} 2 \\ \times 8 \\ \hline \end{array}$$

15

$$\begin{array}{r} 6 \\ \times 5 \\ \hline \end{array}$$

16

$$\begin{array}{r} 10 \\ \times 4 \\ \hline \end{array}$$

17 Circle equal groups. How many groups are there?
How many are left over?

_____ groups _____ left over

Problem Solving

18 Mr. Porter has 45 pieces of wood.
He stacks the wood in 5 equal piles.
How many pieces of wood are in each pile?

_____ pieces

Name ______________________________

Here Kitty, Kitty

Allan saw some kittens at the pet store. He decided to find out how many there were in all.

- The kittens were in groups of 5.
- There were more than 18 kittens in the store.

Use both addition and multiplication to show how many kittens could have been in the store.

Show your work.

Name ______________________________

Calculator • Addition, Subtraction, and Place Value

Start with 435.

Which numbers can you add and still have 4 hundreds?

45	55	65

Use a .

Press AC 4 3 5 + 4 5 = .

Write the answer 480

Press AC 4 3 5 + 5 5 = .

Write the answer ______

Press AC 4 3 5 + 6 5 = .

Write the answer ______

So, you can add 45 and 55 and still have 4 hundreds.

Practice and Problem Solving

Use a . Circle the numbers.

1. Which can you *add* to 347 and still have 3 hundreds?

   23 81 48 39 65 92 52 19 70

2. Which can you *subtract* from 568 and still have 5 hundreds?

   19 25 45 82 68 30 96 73 57

Name ________________________________

Problem Solving on Location

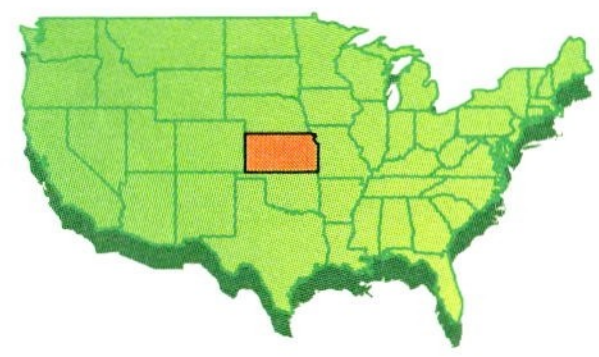

At the Fair

At the Kansas State Fair, you can go on exciting rides, enjoy special foods, and see many interesting things.

You have $7.00 to spend at the fair. How do you spend it?

State Fair Prices	
Entrance Fee	$2.00
Ferris Wheel	$.50
Petting Zoo	$1.00
Pony Ride	$1.00
Lunch	$1.50

Complete the chart.

Activity	Price	Total Spent
Entrance Fee	$2.00	$2.00

Name ______________________

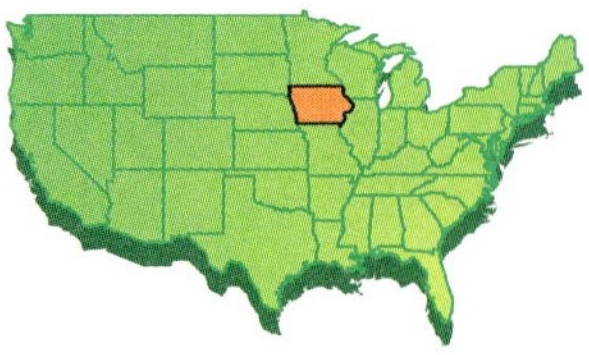

PROBLEM SOLVING ON LOCATION

On the Farm

Iowa is the "corn capital" of our country. More corn is grown in Iowa than in any other state.

How many different ways can you put 12 corn plants into more than one row?

Use ●.
Draw to show each way you find.
Write the numbers.

_____ rows
_____ in each row

_____ rows
_____ in each row

_____ rows
_____ in each row

_____ rows
_____ in each row

PICTURE GLOSSARY

A.M. (page 137)
The time between midnight and noon.

add (page 3)

2 + 4 = 6

addend (page 3)

↓ ↓
5 + 2 = 7

after (page 63)

30 comes **after** 29.

29, **30**

bar graph (page 77)

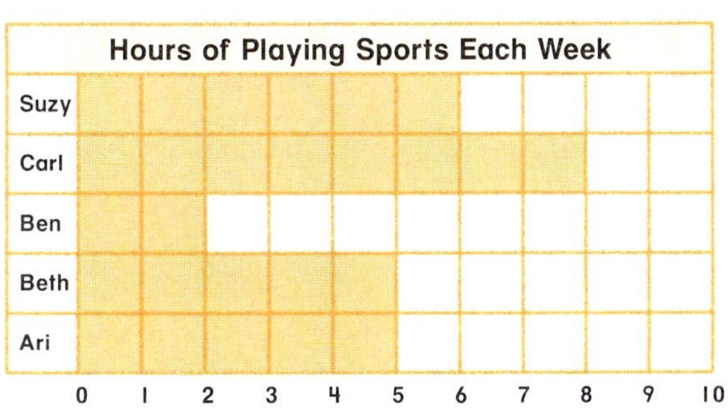

before (page 63)

39, 40

39 comes **before** 40.

between (page 63)

19, **20,** 21

20 comes **between** 19 and 21.

calendar (page 141)

November						
S	M	Tu	W	Th	F	S
		1	2	3	4	5
6	7	8	9	10	11	12
13	14	15	16	17	18	19
20	21	22	23	24	25	26
27	28	29	30			

centimeter (page 275)

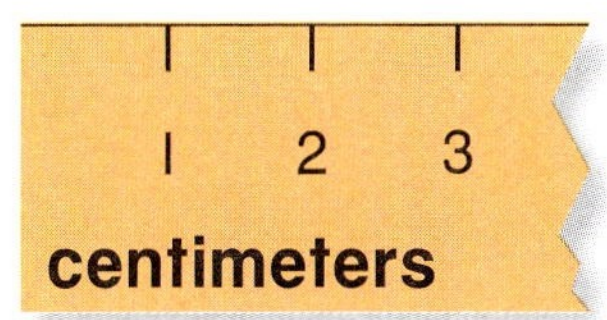

circle (page 241)

cone (page 257)

congruent figures (page 245)

Figures with the same size and shape are **congruent**.

corner (page 243)

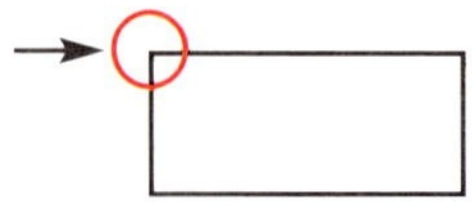

a **corner** of a plane shape

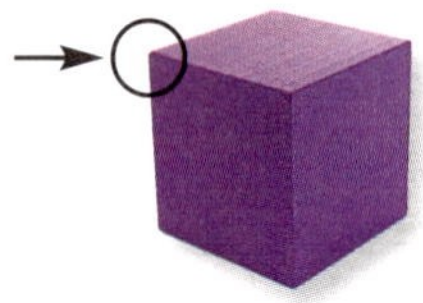

a **corner** of a solid figure

count back (page 21)

7 − 3 = ?

Start at 7. Count back 3.

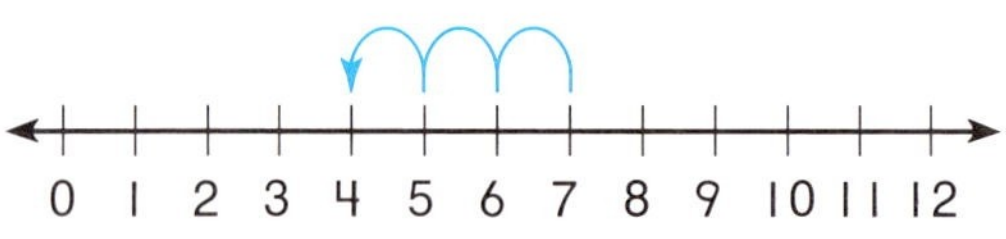

6, 5, **4**

7 − 3 = 4

count on (page 5)

3 + 2 = ?

Start at 3. Count on 2.

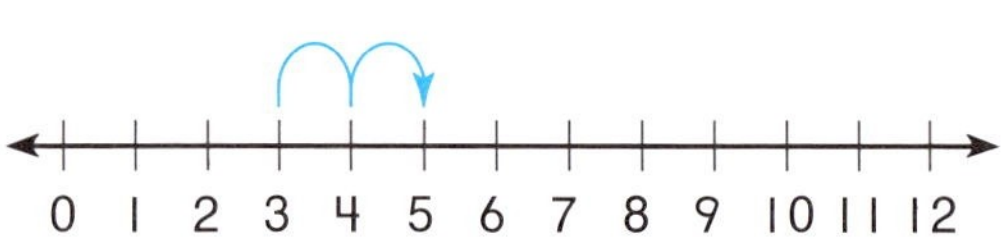

4, **5**

3 + 2 = 5

cube (page 257)

cup (page 285)

cylinder (page 257)

difference (page 21)

6 − 4 = **2**

↑ difference

digit (page 49)

digit → 51 ← digit

51 has two **digits.**

dime (page 97)

10¢

10 cents

divide (page 436)

$12 \div 3 = 4$

dollar (page 103)

dollar sign → $1.00 one dollar

↑ decimal point

doubles (page 7)

$3 + 3 = 6$

doubles plus one (page 7)

$3 + 4 = 7$

edge (page 261)

edge →

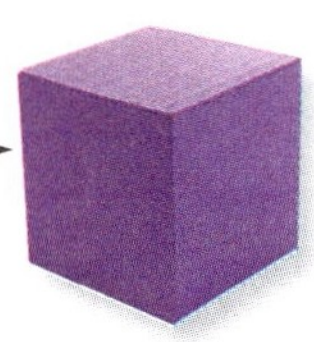

equal groups (page 411)

3 groups of 2

$2 + 2 + 2 = 6$

equal parts (page 335)

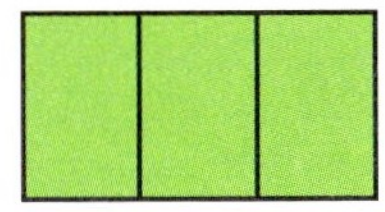

The parts of this rectangle are equal.

equal sign (page 3)

$3 + 1 = 4$

↑ equal sign

equal to (page 61)

25 = 25

estimate (page 177)

about 10 buttons

even numbers (page 65)

0, 2, 4, 6, 8, 10 . . .

face (page 259)

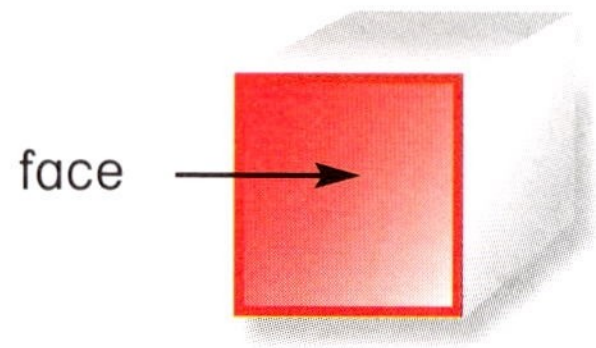

fact family (page 25)

6 + 7 = 13   7 + 6 = 13

13 − 6 = 7   13 − 7 = 6

flip (page 249)

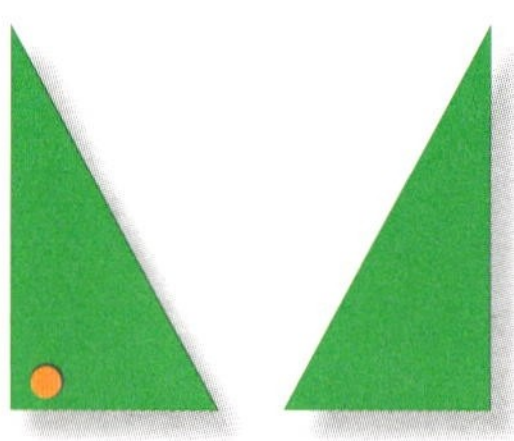

foot (page 273)

A **foot** is 12 inches.

fractions (page 337)

one-half   one-third   one-fourth   one-sixth

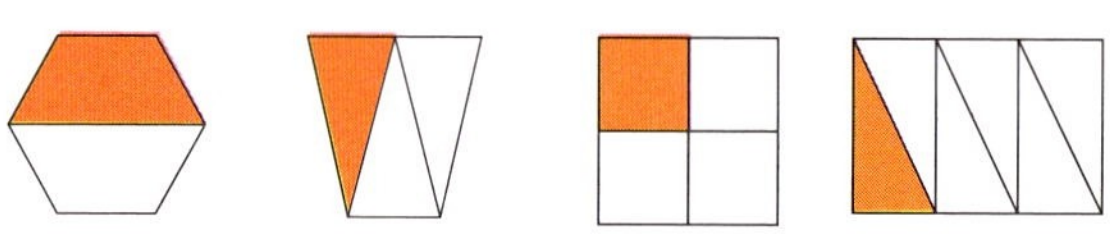

$\frac{1}{2}$ $\frac{1}{3}$ $\frac{1}{4}$ $\frac{1}{6}$

gram (page 291)

This clip weighs about 1 gram.

greater than > (page 61)

63 is **greater than** 29.

63 > 29

half-dollar (page 99)

50¢   50 cents

half-hour (page 125)

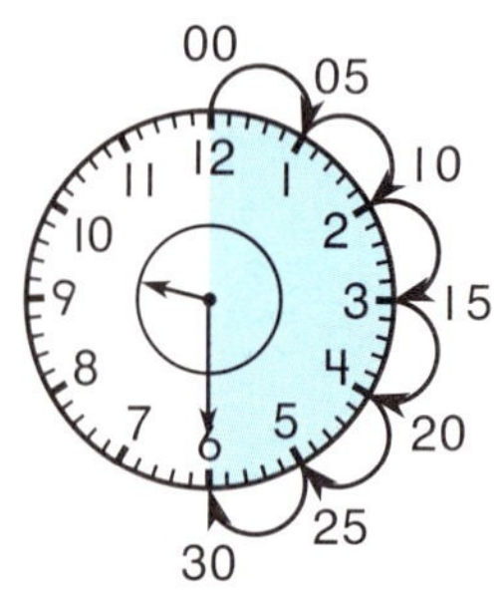

hour (page 125)

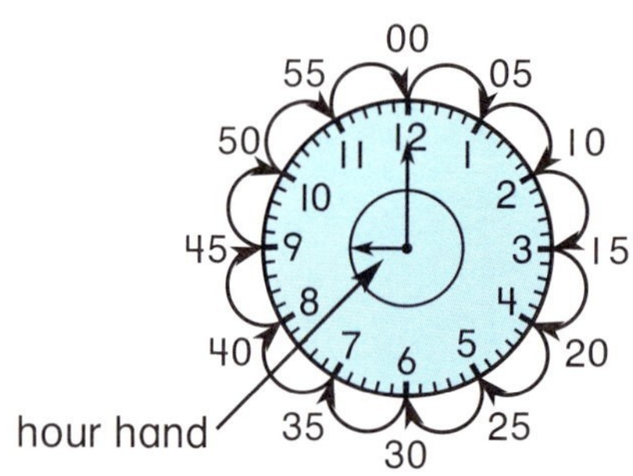

hundreds (page 307)

2 **hundreds**

200

inch (page 271)

kilogram (page 291)

This book weighs about
1 **kilogram**.

less than < (page 61)

29 is **less than** 63.

29 < 63

line of symmetry (page 245)

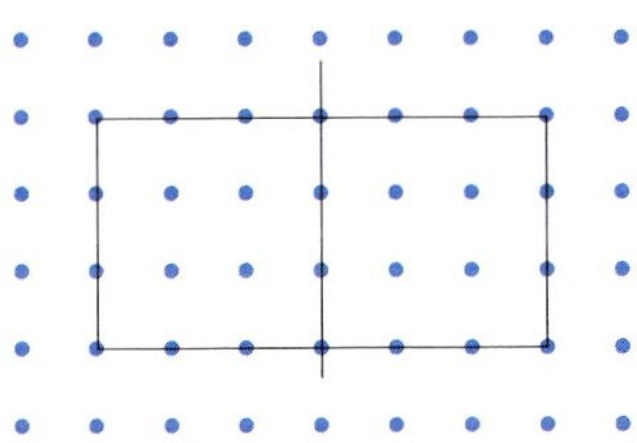

liter (page 287)

A **liter** is a little more than a quart.

meter (page 275)

A **meter** is 100 centimeters.

minutes (page 125)

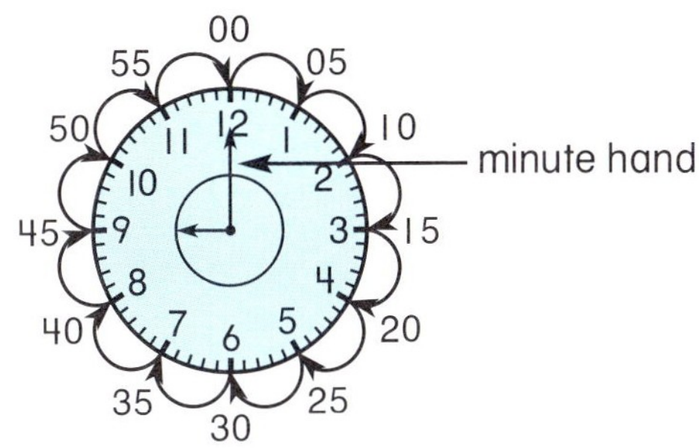

multiplication sentence
(page 417)

$4 \times 3 = 12$

multiply (page 413)

$2 \times 3 = \mathbf{6}$ ← product

nickel (page 97)

5¢ 5 cents

number sentence (page 13)

$6 + 8 = 14$

odd numbers (page 65)

1, 3, 5, 7, 9, 11 . . .

ones (page 45)

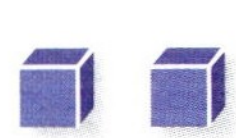

2 **ones**

order property (page 3)

$6 + 3 = 9$

$3 + 6 = 9$

ordinal numbers (page 59)

first **second** **third**

ounce (page 289)

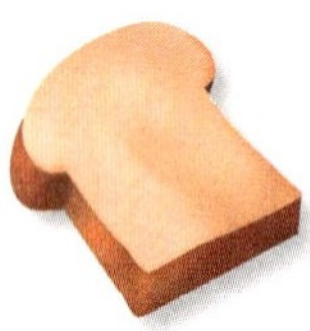

This weighs about 1 **ounce**.

oval (page 241)

P.M. (page 137)

The time between noon and midnight.

pattern (page 69)

30, 40, 50, 60, 70 . . .

Count by tens.

penny (page 97)

1¢ 1 cent

perimeter (page 277)

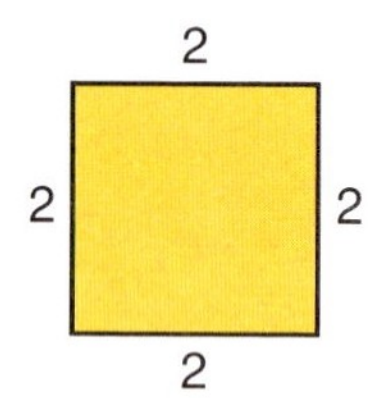

$2 + 2 + 2 + 2 = 8$

pictograph (page 85)

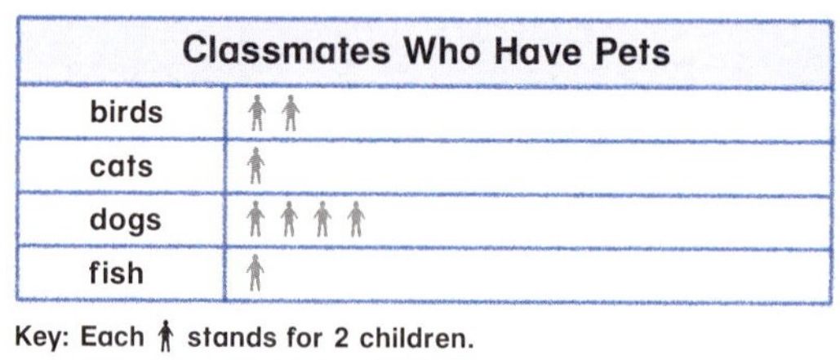

picture graph (page 75)

pint (page 285)

2 cups = 1 **pint**

pound (page 289)

This weighs 1 **pound**.

pyramid (page 257)

quart (page 285)

4 cups = 1 **quart**

quarter (page 99)

25¢

25 cents

rectangle (page 241)

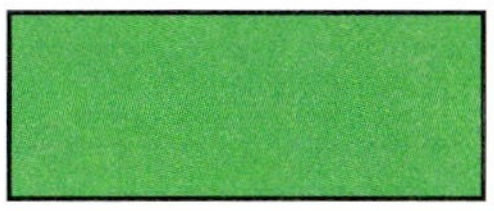

rectangular prism (page 257)

regroup (page 161)

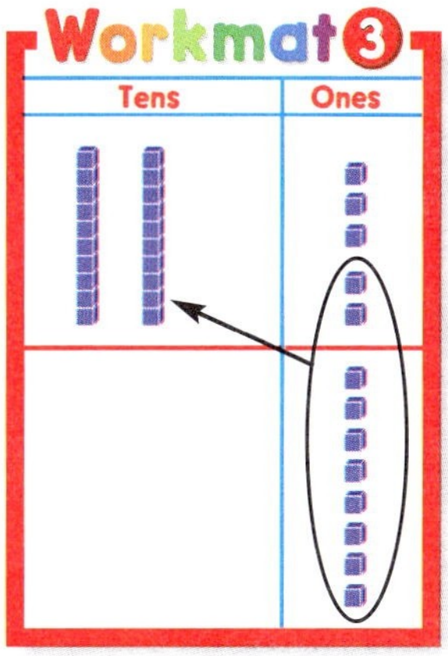

round (page 177)

To estimate to the closest ten.

18 is closer to 20.

side (page 243)

skip-count (page 67)

5, 10, 15, 20, 25 . . .

slide (page 251)

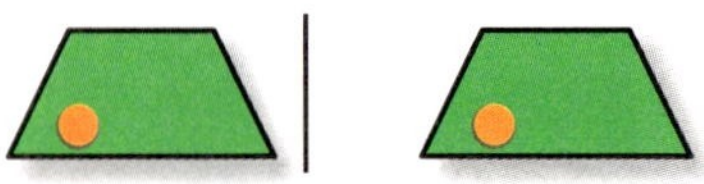

sphere (page 257)

square (page 241)

subtract (page 19)

$6 - 2 = 4$

sum (page 3)

$6 + 9 = 15$ ← **sum**

table (page 79)

Our Favorite Sandwiches	
cheese	III
bologna	𝍸 II
hamburger	𝍸 I
tuna	III

tally marks (page 79)

temperature (page 293)

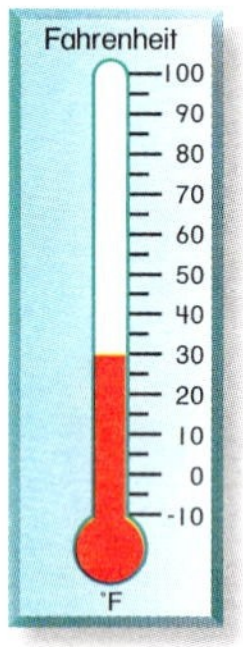

thermometer

The **temperature** is 30°F.

ten frame (page 9)

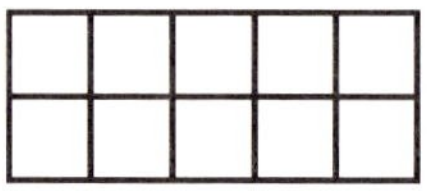

tens (page 45)

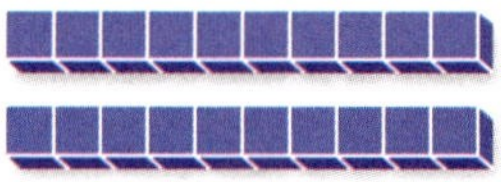

triangle (page 241)

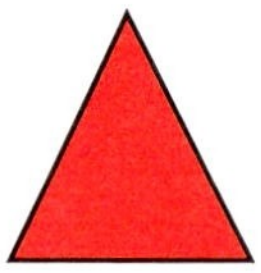

turn (page 249)

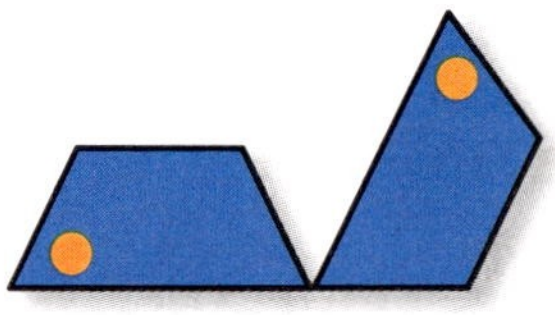

zero property (page 3)

$5 + 0 = 5$

Photography Credits
Page placement key: (t) top, (c) center, (b) bottom, (l) left, (r) right, (bg) background, (i) inset

14 (tc) Doug Perrine/Innerspace Visions; 14 (cb) A. Flowers & L. Newman/Photo Researchers; 14 (b) Doug Perrine/Innerspace Visions; 69 (t) S. L. Craig Jr./Bruce Coleman, Inc.; 70 (c) Jane Burton/Bruce Coleman, Inc.; 93 (l) Bumann/StockFood America; 93 (cl) Zeva Oelbaum/Envision; 93 (cr) (br) Maximillian Stock/StockFood America; 93 (r) Watt/StockFood America; 94a (t) R. Kord/H. Armstrong Roberts; 94a (r) D. Lada/H. Armstrong Roberts; 94a (b) Andy Williams/H. Armstrong Roberts; 94a (l) Lee Snider/Corbis; 94b (tl) S. J. Krasemann/Peter Arnold, Inc.; 94b (tlc) Wayne Nelson; 94b (tcr) Lydia Richardson/Peter Arnold, Inc.; 94b (tr) Tony Arruza/Corbis; 94b (bl) Raymond Gehman/Corbis; 94b (blc) Annie Griffiths/Corbis; 94b (brc) Scott Leonhart/Positive Images; 94b (br) Kim Taylor/Bruce Coleman, Inc.; 143 (tr) Lori Adamski Peek/Tony Stone Images; 143 (br) Melanie Carr/Zephyr Images; 143 (cr) Myrleen Ferguson/PhotoEdit; 144 (tl) Robert Morfey/Tony Stone Images; 144 (tr) Don Smetzer/Tony Stone Images; 154a (tr) Jeff Greenberg/Photo Researchers; 154b (tr) Nawrocki; 238a (tr) D. Logan/H. Armstrong Roberts; 238b (tr) G. Aherns/H. Armstrong Roberts; 302 (c) Priscilla Connell/Index Stock Photography; 304a (tr) Museum of American Folk Art; 304b (tr) Richard Hutchings/Photo Researchers; 366a (tr) Lee Foster/Bruce Coleman, Inc.; 366b (t) Joseph Sohm/Visions of America, LLLC/PictureQuest; 393 (t) William Ferguson/PhotoEdit; 394 (b) Manfred Danegger/Tony Stone Images; 394 (tc) Donald Johnston/Tony Stone Images; 443 (bc) Don Mason/The Stock Market; 453 (t) Ron Kimball Photography; 454a (t) Kansas State Fair; 454b (tr) K. Vreeland/H. Armstrong Roberts.

All other photographs by Harcourt photographers listed below,
© Harcourt: Weronica Ankarorn, John Bateman, Victoria Bowen, Ken Kinzie, Ron Kunzman, Allan Maxwell, Sheri O'Neal, Quebecor Digital Imaging, Sonny Senser, Terry Sinclair.

Illustration Credits

Page: 319, Michelle Angers; 123, Lori Bilter; 425, 426, 427, 428, 429, 430, 431, 432, Ken Bowser; 149, 223, 299, 361, 449, Mark Buehner; 209, 210, 211, 212, 213, 214, 215, 217, 218, Beth Buffington; 21, 23, 24, 26, 28, 237, 238, 453, Annette Cable; 161, 162, 163, Lisa Campbell-Ernst; 169, Tom Casmer; 137, David Christensen; 51, 52, 53, 54, 283, 335, 336, 338, 339, 341, 342, 343, 344, Dave Clegg; 7, 9, 10,12, 13, 23, Mike Dammer; 140, Nick Diggory; 37, 38, 73, Cameron Eagle; 385, 386, 387, 388, 389, 390, 391, 392, 395, Kathi Ember; 98, Len Epstein; 221, 223, 224, 225, 226, 227, 228, Peter Fasolino; 155, Dagmar Fehlau; 239, 241, 242, 249, Nancy Freeman; 91, 92 151, 152, 235, 236, 302, 363, 364, 451, Diane Greenseld; 171, 172, 175, 176, 177, John Gurney; 195, 196, 197, 198, 199, 200, 201, 202, 203, 204, 205, Jean Hirashima; 435, Bob Holt; 75, 77, 78, 83, 84, 85, Linda Howard-Bittner; 95, Barbara Hronilovich; 33, 34, 35, 36, 193, Laura Huliska-Beith; 31, 45, 46, 48, 49, 50, CD Hullinger; 47, 74, 347, Jui Ishida; 33, 289, 290, 293, 295, 296, 297, Mark Jarman; 47, 74, 397, Nathan Jarvis; 135, 137, 138, 139, 140, 141, 142, 143, 144, 145, 146, 257, 258, 261, Larry Jones; 125, 126, 128, 129, 130, 131, Manual King; 183, 184, 185, 186, 187, 188, 189, 190, 191, 349, 350, 351, 352, 353, 354, 355, 356, 357, 359, Terry Kovalcik; 267, Kenneth Laidlaw; 1, 3, 4, 5, 6, 16, 25, 399, 400, 401, 402, 403, 404, Chis Lensch; 409, Barbara Lipp; 17, 287, 290, 293, 295, 296, 298, 307, 308, 309, 310, 311, 312, 313, 314, 315, 316, 317, Dan McGeehan; Welcome Pages, Deborah Melmon; 285, 286, 287, 288, 291, 292, Cheryl Mendenhall; 266, Daniel Moreton; 321, 322, 329, 330, Keiko Motoyama; 57, Michelle Noiset; 192, 411, 412, 413, 414, 415, 416, 417, 418, 419, 420, Tim Raglin; 50, 53, 54, Chris Reed; 181, Barry Rockwell; 323, 324, 326, 327, 328, Bob Shein; 305, Roni Shepard; 98, 101, 102, 105, 106, Andrew Shiff; 432, Remy Simard; 97, 99, 100, 103, 104, Tammy Smith; 61, 62, 63, 67, 68, 357, Jackie Snider; 90, 109, 111, 112, 113, 114, 115, 116, 118, 119, 120, 150, 234, 300, 362, 450, Ken Spengler; 335, 337, 338, 339, 340, 341, 342, 343, 344, Steve Sullivan; 333, Gary Taxali; 76, 79, 80, 81, 82, 243, 244, Terry Taylor; 367, Kat Thacker; 269, 270, 272, 273, 274, 275, 276, 278, 279, 280, Gary Torrisi; 19, 94, 153, 154, 303, 304, 365, 366, Baker Vail; 60, 64, 65, 66, 70, 243, 244, 245, 247, 248, 251, 252, Sally Vitsky; 369, 370, 371, 372, 373, 374, 375, 376, 377, 378, 379, 380, Sam Ward; 126, 127, 132, Tom Ward; 383, Shari Warren; 255, Mike Wohnoutka; 157, 158, 159, 160, 164, 207, 437, 438, 439, 440, 441, 442, 444, 445, Jason Wolff.